11/06

P9-DUS-093

THE GLORIOUS SOUPS AND
STEWS OF ITALY

THE GLORIOUS
SOUPS AND STEWS
OF ITALY

BY DOMENICA MARCHETTI

PHOTOGRAPHS BY William Meppem

CHRONICLE BOOKS

SAN FRANCISCO

Text copyright © 2006 by Domenica Marchetti.

Photographs copyright © 2006 by
William Meppem.

All rights reserved. No part of this book
may be reproduced in any form without written
permission from the publisher.

Library of Congress Cataloging-in-Publication
Data available.

ISBN-10: 0-8118-4817-5
ISBN-13: 978-0-8118-4817-6
Manufactured in China.

Designed by Beverly Joel
Prop styling by Andy Harris
Food styling by Hannah Dodds

Distributed in Canada by Raincoast Books
9050 Shaughnessy Street
Vancouver, British Columbia V6P 6E5

10 9 8 7 6 5 4 3 2 1

Chronicle Books LLC
85 Second Street
San Francisco, California 94105

www.chroniclebooks.com

DEDICATION

This book is dedicated to my parents,
Gabriella and Francis Marchetti, who made sure
I was well read and well fed;

And to Scott, Nick, and Adriana, my generous and
supportive family, whom I love to feed.

ACKNOWLEDGMENTS

This book would surely have stayed inside my head were it not for some wonderful people. I am indebted to:

Bill LeBlond, my editor at Chronicle Books, for believing in this project from the beginning.

Diane Morgan, my dear friend and the angel on my shoulder throughout the entire process.

Antonia Allegra, whose Symposium for Professional Food Writers at the Greenbrier brought me together with the previous two and with Barbara Lauterbach, whose advice helped me get started.

At Chronicle Books, Sharon Silva for her top-notch editing; Amy Treadwell, for keeping things on track; and Beverly Joel, whose design so beautifully captures the text.

Family and friends who took the time to test, taste, and critique the recipes in this book: Maria Marchetti, Anette Emery, Tom Greenwood, Alice Reid, Kimberley Ferlazzo-Ricci, and Miss Liz and Cousin Bob.

Michelle Andonian, for her friendship, gracious hospitality, and superb camera work.

Uncle Darren and Uncle John, for their support.

My father, Francis, for planning all those great trips to Italy around food and wine; and my mother, Gabriella, whose knowledge of and passion for true Italian home cooking have been my single biggest inspiration.

And finally, to my children, Nick and Adriana, who understood that they came first even when it sometimes seemed the book did; and especially to my husband, Scott, for keeping his day job. I am one lucky girl.

Contents

9   INTRODUCTION
Seasonal Soups and Stews at
the Italian Table

13   CHAPTER I
ESSENTIALS
Equipment
Techniques
Ingredients
Recipes

35   CHAPTER 2
Autunno
Recipes for Fall

65   CHAPTER 3
Inverno
Recipes for Winter

95   CHAPTER 4
Primavera
Recipes for Spring

121   CHAPTER 5
Estate
Recipes for Summer

147   CHAPTER 6
ACCOMPANIMENTS
Perfect Partners and
Four Perfect Endings

163   SOURCES

164   INDEX

168   TABLE OF EQUIVALENTS

Introduction

SEASONAL SOUPS AND STEWS
AT THE ITALIAN TABLE

Not long ago I moved with my family to a new house, and the first thing I did was unpack the kitchen. The second was to put on a big pot of lentil soup, a soup that my Italian mother made often when I was growing up and that is still one of my favorites. I did it without much consideration, as if I had no other tasks at hand (such as unpacking my kids' rooms, setting up my computer so I could work, or stripping the acres of floral wallpaper that surrounded us on all sides).

Looking back, it's easy to see what I was trying to accomplish: I was looking for a quick way to turn an unfamiliar place, a place that until a few weeks earlier had been inhabited by an entirely different family, into a home for my family.

It worked. Before long the house was filled with the fragrance of onions, vegetables, and bay leaf. It smelled like an Italian kitchen, and to me that meant home. And all I had actually invested was a few minutes in assembling and chopping the ingredients and adding them to the pot.

There is no better aromatherapy than a homemade soup or stew simmering on the stove. Just the thought that dinner is virtually cooking itself is a great comfort to all of us who love the idea of a home-cooked meal but don't have endless hours to spend in the kitchen. And while fall and winter are the seasons when most people turn their attention to soups and stews, I find I crave them all year long. To me, a bowl of smooth, sweet red pepper and tomato soup, or a light stew of fresh tuna and cannellini beans, is perfect summer fare, just as appetizing as—if not more than—anything you might cook on the grill.

Italian cooks are masters of the art of conjuring soups and stews for any season. While pasta may be Italy's most recognized culinary contribution, soups and stews form the backbone of Italian home cooking and exemplify what everyone loves best about Italian food: the use of in-season herbs and vegetables and uncomplicated cooking techniques that let the ingredients do the work.

What makes these dishes especially appealing is that they rarely call for exotic or expensive ingredients. Italians are great at spinning the most meager components into a spectacular dish. Who would think that a handful of bread sticks, a few ladlefuls of broth, and a little sheep's milk cheese could be transformed into an elegant soup fit for a fall dinner party?

On the other hand, Italians also know how to indulge themselves. Rich osso buco (braised veal shank) is expensive to make when the star ingredient is upward of ten dollars a pound. But, believe me, it is well worth the splurge once in a while, especially in winter.

Italians take a wonderfully broad view of what makes a soup or a stew. There are more than a half dozen names to describe soups alone—aquacotta, brodo, minestra, vellutata, and zuppa among them—depending on whether the finished dish is a broth, a purée, a thick porridge, or something in between.

Stews are just as diverse and prized. Pellegrino Artusi, Italy's revered nineteenth-century authority on gastronomy, called stews "the most appetizing dishes" in his famous collection of recipes, La scienza in cucina e l'arte di mangiar bene. There are spezzatini and stracotti, long-simmered wintry one-pot meals that are similar to what Americans typically think of as stew. But Italians also use stewing techniques for simmering smaller cuts of meat or fish in salsa (in sauce) and for bringing out the best of the season's vegetables, cooking them in umido (braised), with aromatic herbs and just enough liquid to coax out and intensify their flavors.

Most soups and stews are easy to make, can be prepared ahead of time, and are often better when made in advance and then reheated. There are plenty of recipes like that in this book. But they are not all so carefree, nor would I want them to be. There is something deeply satisfying and therapeutic about spending a morning or an afternoon in the kitchen, perhaps with a friend or a child, rolling out silky sheets of pasta dough and making hand-cut noodles, or filling and shaping cappelletti for cooking in homemade broth. I would be bored silly if I didn't have a good kitchen project to challenge me every so often.

Although I have been cooking since I was tall enough to see over the kitchen counter, I am a newspaper reporter by training, so that is how I approached the Glorious Soups and Stews of Italy: I dug around and did a lot of research. I traveled to Italy and ate soup and stew for lunch and dinner day after day (admittedly, quite happily). I pulled out my mother's old cookbooks and her extensive stash of Italian cooking magazines dating back to the early 1960s. I queried my mother, a superb cook, about her own favorite soup and stew recipes, which she generously shared with me.

The result is this collection of my favorite seasonal recipes for soups and stews. I have included vanishing classics and antique recipes that deserve to be revived, regional specialties, treasured family recipes handed down to me from my grandmother, mother, and aunts, and contemporary recipes that I created in my own kitchen.

The opening chapter, Essentials, contains helpful information on equipment and techniques, details on ingredients used in the book, and recipes for broths, sauces, and fresh egg pasta. Tips, variations, and more information are included in the Cook's Note at the end of many of the recipes.

The recipe chapters are divided by season, beginning with autunno (fall) and ending with estate (summer). Within each chapter, the recipes reflect the following order: broth-based soups, smooth and creamy soups, hearty soups, fish and shellfish stews, poultry and meat stews, and vegetable stews. Most of the stews, and many of the soups, are intended as main-dish courses. Some of the lighter, broth-based soups are intended as first courses, and a number of the vegetable stews are ideal side dishes. These various roles are noted in the individual recipes. You should, of course, feel free to make and serve the recipes as you like, however. Indeed, sometimes a bowl of braised greens or a light brothy soup might be all you want or need to eat.

In Accompaniments, the final chapter, you will find recipes for perfect partners for soups and stews, including risotto, polenta, bruschetta, and crostini. And because I like the idea of ending on a sweet note, I also have included four recipes for seasonal crostate, rustic dessert tarts.

While writing this book, I was asked many times if I have a favorite soup or stew recipe. The answer is that I can't possibly choose from among them. But if there is one dish that I have prepared for myself more than any other, it is without a doubt a simple bowl of pastina (tiny pasta) cooked in broth. I have been eating pastina since I began eating solid food, and I am sure I could have it every day for the rest of my life without ever tiring of it. I like it best made with homemade broth, but more often than not I use canned broth, bouillon cubes, or even water flavored with butter, salt, and Parmigiano-Reggiano cheese. It is easy to make and always delicious: For one person, bring 2 cups broth to a boil, slowly pour in ⅓ to ½ cup pastina—acini di pepe (peppercorns), stelline (little stars), and annellini (little rings) are my favorite shapes—reduce the heat, and let the soup simmer, stirring occasionally, until the pastina is fully cooked. Pour the soup into a bowl and sprinkle with lots of freshly grated Parmigiano-Reggiano. Buon appetito.

CHAPTER I

ESSENTIALS

14   EQUIPMENT

16   TECHNIQUES

18   INGREDIENTS

RECIPES

24   Brodo di Pollo
Homemade Chicken Broth

25   Sostanzioso Brodo di Manzo
Rich Roasted Beef Broth

26   Brodo di Carne
Homemade Meat Broth

27   Brodo di Magro
Homemade Vegetable Broth

28   Salsa Fresca di Pomodoro
Fresh Tomato Sauce

30   Salsa Semplice di Pomodoro
Basic Tomato Sauce

31   Pasta all'Uovo
Fresh Egg Pasta Dough

EQUIPMENT

You don't need a lot of fancy equipment to make great soups and stews. In fact, you probably have most of what you need already. Following is an alphabetical list of tools and equipment that I have found useful in making the recipes in this book.

BAKING SHEETS

For making *bruschetta* and *crostini*, and for roasting peppers. Select heavy-gauge rimmed sheets.

BLENDER

For puréeing smooth and creamy soups and some sauces.

BOWLS

For individual servings of soups and stews. In general, I prefer shallow, rimmed soup plates for both soups and stews. Many soups and stews are ladled over bread, rice, or polenta, all nicely accommodated in one of these shallow bowls, and the wide mouth provides a good-sized area for drizzling olive oil or sprinkling cheese on top.

CHEESECLOTH

For straining solids from broths and for removing grit from dried porcini mushroom soaking liquid. I prefer unbleached cheesecloth, which I rinse in cold water and wring out before using.

COLANDER

For draining pasta and, when lined with cheesecloth, for straining solids from broth.

DUTCH OVEN

This big pot is what I use to cook most of my soups and stews. It has a tight-fitting lid, a heavy, flat bottom that is ideal for sautéing aromatic vegetables and browning meat in one layer, and it can be used on both the stove top and in the oven. A 5½-quart Dutch oven made from enameled cast iron is best.

FINE-MESH SIEVE

For removing grit from dried porcini mushroom soaking liquid and from shellfish stews, for straining vegetable broth and some soups to rid them of fibers, and for adding flour to sautéed aromatics.

FOOD MILL WITH MULTIPLE PLATES

For removing seeds from and puréeing canned tomatoes and for puréeing roasted vegetables.

FOOD PROCESSOR

For making pasta dough and pastry dough, making fresh bread crumbs, chopping vegetables, puréeing some soups and vegetable mixtures, puréeing tomato sauce, and mixing stuffing for *cappelletti*.

FREEZER CONTAINERS

Sturdy plastic containers in a variety of sizes (1- and 2-quart capacity) for freezing sauces, soups and stews, and stocks.

GARLIC PRESS

For puréeing whole peeled garlic cloves. A number of recipes call for making a paste of garlic and salt, which is used to add flavor to soup and stew bases. The garlic press makes fast work of this step.

GRATER

Microplane makes a grater-zester with fine rasps that is good for grating hard cheeses, such as *Parmigiano-Reggiano* and pecorino, and the zest of lemons and other citrus fruits. The finest holes on a box grater work as well. I use the large holes on a box grater to make *pasta grattata* (page 71).

KNIVES

You need to do a fair amount of chopping when you make soups and stews. I use a paring knife for trimming and peeling, a 6-inch stainless-steel chef's knife for chopping and for crushing garlic cloves, and a serrated knife for slicing bread.

PEPPER MILL

For seasoning soups and stews with freshly ground black pepper.

POTATO MASHER

For breaking up canned whole tomatoes.

SAUCEPAN OR SAUCEPOT

A 4-quart lidded pot (a saucepan has a single long handle, a saucepot has a pair of short handles) made of stainless steel or another nonreactive material, for making sauces and for simmering some broth-based and other soups.

SAUTÉ PAN WITH LID

For various uses, including browning chicken, meat, and fish; sautéing vegetables; and cooking shellfish.

SKILLET

A small (8- to 9-inch) skillet for frying

or sautéing aromatics and finely
chopped pancetta and prosciutto, and
for making *crespelle*; and a large (12- to
14-inch) skillet for sautéing vegetables.

SKIMMER
For removing foam from the surface of
simmering broths and soups.

SOUP TUREEN
While not a necessity, a decorative
soup tureen is a nice way to serve soup,
or even stew, to company.

SPATTER SCREEN
To minimize messes (and spatter
burns) while browning meat.

SPOONS, SPATULAS, AND OTHER STIRRING UTENSILS
An assortment of wooden spoons and
spatulas is useful for stirring sautéing
vegetables and aromatics and for
deglazing. I use a slotted metal spoon
for removing crisped or cooked
ingredients (such as diced pancetta)
from a pan and leaving behind the fat; a
rubber spatula for scraping out mixing
bowls, the work bowl of the food
processor, and the blender pitcher; and
a heatproof rubber spatula for stirring
some hot mixtures.

STOCKPOT
A tall, narrow 12-quart pot for making
meat-based broths.

TONGS
For turning pieces of meat during
browning.

TECHNIQUES

Before you begin to cook, read through the whole recipe and set out all the ingredients you will need. Do any prep work, such as trimming, chopping, and grating, in advance, so that you won't have to scramble to get it done when the time comes to add the ingredient to your soup or stew. Here are the primary prep techniques you will need to know, from how to peel and seed tomatoes to how to clean mussels, followed by brief explanations of the most common techniques that come into play once you start cooking.

CHOPPING

Many of the recipes in this book start with the chopping of aromatic vegetables and herbs, particularly carrots, celery, onions, garlic, and parsley. These ingredients, either alone or in combination, are the essential flavor base for many Italian soups and stews. These should always be finely chopped, unless a recipe specifies otherwise.

PEELING AND SEEDING TOMATOES

There are two simple ways to peel tomatoes. For the first one, bring a large pot of water to a vigorous boil. Using a sharp paring knife, lightly score an X into the flower end of each tomato. Carefully plunge the tomatoes, no more than 2 to 4 at a time, into the boiling water and leave for 15 to 30 seconds— no longer or the tomatoes will start to cook and you will lose flesh when you peel them. With a slotted spoon, transfer the tomatoes to a colander and rinse briefly with cold water. The skins will now peel off easily with the paring knife.

The second method is the one I prefer. It takes a little longer, but is

done without subjecting the tomatoes to heat first. Slice off the stem end of the tomato with a paring knife. Then, using a vegetable peeler, pare off the skin in strips.

To seed the peeled tomatoes, cut them in half through the stem end and cut out the core. Then cut them once more, into quarters, and remove the seeds by pushing them out with your fingers. You can then chop the tomatoes as directed.

CLEANING AND STORING CLAMS AND MUSSELS

Live clams and mussels will keep for a day or two in the refrigerator, but I always use them the same day I buy them. Store clams and mussels uncovered in the refrigerator on a bed of ice, or with ice scattered around them in a bowl. Do not keep them in plastic or immersed in water for any length of time, or they will suffocate. Much of the shellfish available these days is farm raised and therefore contains less dirt and grit than shellfish harvested from the wild.

To clean clams and mussels, scrub their shells with a stiff brush under cold running water. Discard any that do not close tightly when handled. If the mussels have beards, the fibrous tufts they use to hold on to pilings and rocks, you need to remove them. Using a towel or just your fingers, grasp the beard gently but firmly and yank it toward the shell's hinge. This will remove the fibers without tearing the mussel meat itself.

Just before cooking, you can soak clams and mussels in cold water to cover to which you have added a sprinkle of

cornmeal. Let them sit for 20 to 30 minutes. As they breathe and filter water, they will expel any grit trapped inside their shells. Drain and rinse thoroughly after soaking.

PEELING AND DEVEINING SHRIMP

I use a curved metal tool known as a shrimp peeler and deveiner to make quick work of this task. Insert the pointed end of the deveiner into the head end of the shrimp and push it through the tail end. Gently lift up to pull away the shrimp shell. The black veinlike tract that runs the length of the back should lift out, too; if not, pull it off with your fingers and discard. Rinse the shrimp under cold running water and dry thoroughly; store them in a container in your refrigerator until you are ready to use them.

MARINATING

A few recipes in this book call for marinating meat or fish overnight in liquid and aromatic herbs and vegetables before cooking. This process gives all the flavors a chance to mingle and infuse the main ingredient, adding depth to the finished dish.

SAUTÉING

The first step in cooking a soup or stew is often sautéing the chopped aromatics in a small amount of fat, usually a good-quality olive oil. It is usually done over medium heat, so that the vegetables soften but do not turn brown, and often requires frequent stirring with a wooden spoon so that the ingredients cook evenly. It is especially important not to let garlic brown, or it will be bitter.

BROWNING

Stews featuring meat and poultry usually call first for browning the meat in a small amount of oil over medium-high heat. Heat the oil before you add the meat so that the surface of the meat will begin to sear and brown immediately. Browning caramelizes the natural sugars in the meat, enhancing its flavor and its appearance. Give the meat at least 2 to 3 minutes to form a brown crust before checking or turning it with tongs; if you try to turn the meat too early, you may tear it. If you are browning chunks of meat for stew, do not crowd the pan or the meat will steam rather than brown; instead, brown the meat in batches that give the pieces plenty of room.

DEGLAZING

This step typically takes place directly after browning meat or sautéing vegetables. Raise the heat to medium-high or high before pouring in a small amount of liquid, usually wine or broth. The liquid should begin to bubble almost immediately. As it does, use a wooden spoon or spatula to scrape any browned bits off the bottom of the pan; these dislodged bits carry flavor.

SIMMERING

After deglazing, more liquid, usually broth, water, or tomato purée or sauce, is added to the pot. Once it begins to boil, reduce the heat to medium-low, so that the soup or stew will cook gently but steadily. You may want to cover the pot, either partially or completely, at this point, depending on how thick you want the liquid to be when the dish is finished cooking.

BRAISING

Slow cooking large, tough cuts of browned meat in a small amount of liquid over low heat is known as braising. In Italian, the process is sometimes referred to as *in umido*, or as *stracotto*, literally "overcooked." Braising produces a richly flavored sauce and succulent, fork-tender meat. Vegetables can also be braised. Hearty greens such as kale, rapini, and chard are particularly good cooked this way and then drizzled with a little fresh olive oil at serving time.

STEWING

In general, stews call for less liquid than soup, but more than a braise. For meat stews, tough but flavorful cuts of meat are sliced into bite-sized pieces, browned, and then simmered in liquid to create a saucy broth. Seafood stews usually call for a mix of shellfish and meaty white fish, such as monkfish. Vegetable stews, meanwhile, can be light and quick, featuring fresh in-season vegetables, or hearty and long simmered, with beans and legumes added for body.

ADDING CREAM TO SOUPS

When a recipe calls for adding cream toward the end of cooking, be sure that the cream is at room temperature or slightly warm before pouring it into the hot soup, and be sure that the soup is not boiling. Pouring cold cream into boiling liquid may cause the cream to curdle. Bring the soup to a simmer, rather than a boil, once the cream has been added.

SEASONING

Salt and freshly ground black pepper, as well as ground cayenne pepper, are often added to taste. Start with a small amount and then add more as needed.

STORING

Most soups and stews can be stored in airtight containers in the refrigerator for up to 3 days and in the freezer for longer. Do not freeze soups or stews that contain milk or cream, cooked pasta, or seafood.

REHEATING

Many soups and stews improve in flavor after sitting for several hours or even after being refrigerated overnight and then reheated. Reheat over low heat, adding a little water or broth if necessary to loosen to achieve the proper consistency. This step is especially necessary for soups and stews with beans and other legumes, which continue to absorb liquid even after cooking.

INGREDIENTS

Thanks to the enduring popularity of Italian food and cooking, it is easier than ever before to find genuine, good-quality Italian ingredients in supermarkets and specialty-food shops across the United States. Following is a list of ingredients used in recipes in this book. See Sources (page 163) for mail-order retailers.

ANCHOVIES

Good preserved anchovies are neither fishy nor gray. They are instead meaty and add zest and depth to sauces. You can buy anchovies packed either in salt or in oil. The anchovies I use almost exclusively are Rizzoli brand *alici in salsa piccante*. The small, rectangular red-and-gold tins are packed with rolled anchovy fillets marinated in a savory, slightly spicy olive oil sauce flavored with tuna. Before they were available in the United States, my mother would bring stacks of tins back from Italy, stashing them in the corners of suitcases. Although they are still not widely available here, you can order them online (see Sources). In their absence, use the best-quality anchovy fillets in olive oil that you can find. You can also use anchovies packed in salt, but you will need to fillet them and rinse them well in cold running water to remove excess salt.

ARBORIO RICE

This pearly white, short-grain rice, grown primarily in the Lombardy and Piedmont regions and widely available in shops outside of Italy, is used to make risotto. It has a high starch content, which is what gives risotto its characteristic creamy texture. Carnaroli and Vialone Nano are two other types suitable for risotto, though they are less commonly found.

BEANS AND OTHER LEGUMES

Legumes are used in abundance in Italian soups. A particular soup might be based on a single type, or it can include a mix. Dried legumes, such as *cannellini*, *borlotti*, fava, kidney beans, and chickpeas, should be soaked overnight in abundant cold water to soften them and decrease their cooking time. Dried split peas and lentils do not need to be soaked, as they cook fairly quickly in water or broth. In the fall, cranberry beans, similar to Italian *borlotti* beans, are available fresh in their pods. They can be shelled and cooked without soaking. If you are unable to find fresh cranberry beans, substitute dried ones and soak them overnight before cooking.

BREAD

Good bread is an essential component of many rustic Italian soups. For *crostini*, which are used to garnish soups, I use a thin baguette or a *ficelle* (a long loaf but thinner than the standard baguette) that produces the ideal-sized slices. For *bruschetta* (grilled bread), I use a sturdy country-style loaf, rather than a light, fine-textured one. If bread goes directly into the soup, as in *Zuppa di Magro alla Campagnola* (page 49), I toast it lightly in the oven so that it will retain some texture in the finished soup.

CHESTNUTS

Fresh chestnuts, ideal for roasting, are available in many supermarkets from Thanksgiving through the New Year. They have a rich, sweet flavor and, when cooked, a crumbly texture. You can also buy them precooked and peeled, in cans, jars, or vacuum-packed. For the sake of convenience, I buy the precooked ones for adding to soups and stews. Chestnut flour, made by grinding dried chestnuts, is pale beige and has a sweet, earthy flavor. It adds an unusual sweet note to polenta.

CHICKENS

Look for free-range chickens, preferably organic. They are increasingly available in supermarkets and are much tastier than factory-farm chickens.

EGGS

I use large, organic eggs for all recipes with the exception of two, fresh egg pasta and semolina gnocchi, which call for extra-large eggs.

FARRO

Farro is an ancient whole grain that has been cultivated since Roman times. It is similar in appearance to spelt and wheat berries and, when cooked, has a pleasingly chewy texture and an earthy, nutty flavor. *Farro* is often available in well-stocked supermarkets and Italian food stores. Other whole grains, such as barley, spelt, and wheat berries, may be substituted.

FATBACK

As its name suggests, fatback is the fresh layer of white fat that runs across the back of a pig. It is used in American southern cooking to flavor greens and stews. I use it sparingly in a couple of recipes and, unless you are a vegetarian, I urge you not to leave it out. It adds a

rich flavor to vegetable-based stews. Fatback is sometimes confused with salt pork, the salt-cured fat from the animal's belly, but fatback is uncured and unsalted. Fresh fatback is always creamy white; if it is tinged with yellow it is old and should be discarded. Wrap fatback tightly in plastic and store it in the refrigerator.

FENNEL
Anise-scented fennel is three ingredients in one: a vegetable, an herb, and a spice. The creamy white bulb is crisp and has a mild licorice flavor. It can be sliced or chopped and used raw in salads or cooked in soups and stews. The feathery green tops, similar in appearance to dill, can be chopped and used as a garnish. Fennel seeds have the strongest flavor. Lightly crushed, they add flavor and zest to robust stews.

HERBS
I almost always prefer to cook with fresh herbs rather than dried ones. Their flavor is brighter and is usually nothing like their dried counterparts. The herbs used most frequently in the recipes in this book are basil, bay leaf, flat-leaf parsley, marjoram, oregano, rosemary, and sage.

MARSALA
A fortified, blended wine named for its city of origin in Sicily, Marsala can be sweet, medium-dry, or dry. The recipes in this book call for dry Marsala.

MASCARPONE CHEESE
This rich, double- or triple-cream fresh cow's milk cheese comes from Italy's Lombardy region. The best mascarpone is made from the milk of cows that have been fed a diet of grasses, herbs, and flowers. It has a rich, ivory color and a sweet flavor with a slight acidic tinge. I like to use mascarpone as a garnish on vegetable soups. Crème fraîche, a thick, cultured cream similar to sour cream and tangier than mascarpone, may be substituted.

MEATS
With the exception of veal shanks for *osso buco* (page 88), the best cuts of meat for stews and braises are typically the tougher, less-expensive cuts. I use top round or chuck for beef stews and braises; veal shoulder for most veal stews; lamb shoulder or leg for lamb stews; and, with a couple of exceptions, pork shoulder for pork stews. In every case, look for meat that is free of hormones and antibiotics.

NUTMEG
I prefer freshly grated whole nutmeg to ground nutmeg in a jar because the intense flavor and aroma of the spice deteriorate quickly once it is ground. Use a nutmeg grater, a Microplane grater, or the smallest holes on a box grater to grate nutmeg, and grate only as needed. Store whole nutmeg in a jar with a tight-fitting lid and keep it in a cool, dark place.

OLIVE OIL
All of the recipes in this book call for extra-virgin olive oil, which is made from the first cold pressing of olives and contains less than 1 percent oleic acid. The term *extra virgin* indicates the highest grade of olive oil; however, extra-virgin olive oils can vary considerably in taste, color, and quality. For cooking, I use extra-virgin oil that is light colored and has a mildly fruity flavor. When drizzling raw olive oil over a soup or stew at serving time, I use a darker, more intensely flavored oil. The latter is usually of higher quality and thus more expensive.

PANCETTA
Italian bacon that is cured with salt, pepper, and other spices is known as pancetta. It comes from the belly of the pig and, unlike American bacon, is not smoked. Pancetta is generally rolled up into a large sausage shape for curing and then sold sliced. In the recipes in this book, pancetta is either diced or minced and sautéed with aromatics to add flavor to soups and stews.

PARMIGIANO-REGGIANO CHEESE
This hard, granular grating cheese is used lavishly to flavor Italian soups and stews (or, at least that's how I use it). It has a satisfying robust flavor that is both sharp and rich. You can distinguish it from lesser-quality imitations by the rind, which always has the words *Parmigiano-Reggiano* stamped into it. It is sold in chunks and keeps best tightly wrapped in plastic or foil and refrigerated. For the best flavor, grate it only as needed.

PECORINO ROMANO CHEESE
This aged sheep's milk cheese is paler in color than *Parmigiano-Reggiano* cheese. It has a sharp, salty flavor and is an excellent grating cheese. Buy it in wedges, store it as you would *Parmigiano-Reggiano*, wrapped tightly in plastic or foil and refrigerated, and

grate as needed. I use pecorino in place of *Parmigiano-Reggiano* when I want to punch up the flavor of a finished soup or stew.

POLENTA

Polenta is ground cornmeal. In parts of northern Italy, it replaces pasta as the standard *primo piatto* (first course). Both yellow and white polenta are available but yellow is more common. It can be either finely ground or coarsely ground. My personal preference is coarsely ground yellow polenta. Typically, polenta is cooked in boiling salted water and stirred almost constantly throughout the cooking process. It can be sauced or topped with butter and cheese, or it can be served plain as an accompaniment to stew. Polenta can be cooked to the consistency of a thick porridge, or it can be cooled, sliced, and baked, fried, or grilled. Delicious variations can be made using equal parts cornmeal and buckwheat flour, or equal parts cornmeal and chestnut flour.

PORCINI MUSHROOMS

Fresh porcini mushrooms are fat and meaty and have a subtle woodsy flavor. They are delicious in soups and stews but unfortunately are not easy to find in the United States. Dried porcini are a good substitute. They have a strong, earthy mushroom aroma that adds depth and richness to cold-weather soups and stew. Look for dried porcini mushrooms sold in well-sealed plastic packets. They should be in slices or in large pieces; small bits indicate the mushrooms are old and therefore not as flavorful. Once the packet is opened, store the mushrooms in a zipper-lock plastic bag in the freezer. They will keep indefinitely.

PROSCIUTTO DI PARMA

This imported ham from Parma, Italy, is cured with salt, air-dried, and aged for more than a year. The meat is a deep rose, with creamy white fat. It has a buttery texture and a rich, sweet-salty flavor. Although I like Parma prosciutto best raw, I sometimes use it to add flavor and texture to soups and stews. You can substitute less expensive domestic prosciutto, but it lacks the delicate texture and rich flavor of its imported counterpart.

SAFFRON

Red-gold saffron threads are the dried stigmas of a variety of crocus. The spice is expensive, but only a small pinch is needed to infuse a broth or a sauce with its exotic flavor. You can buy saffron in small amounts, either as threads or as a powder. The powder dissolves more easily, but it is also more easily tampered with. To be sure you are getting pure saffron, buy the threads and either pound them or dissolve them in a little hot liquid before adding to recipes.

SALT

Most table salt has anticaking agents that alter the flavor, so I use either kosher salt or sea salt when cooking (usually whichever one is closer at hand). The sea salt can be either coarse or fine for cooking, but at the table, or when I want to sprinkle a little salt on a finished dish, I always use fine sea salt.

SEMOLINA FLOUR

Pale yellow semolina flour is made from durum (hard) wheat. In Italy, it is used to make pasta, gnocchi, and bread.

TOMATOES

In summer, I buy ripe plum (sometimes labeled Roma) tomatoes at my farmers' market for adding to soups and stews and for making sauce. But when tomatoes are out of season, I prefer canned tomatoes to the flavorless ones found in the produce bin at the super-market. Look for canned whole tomatoes in their natural juices, rather than tomatoes in purée or chopped or diced tomatoes. Some brands of imported San Marzano tomatoes are good, but then again so are some domestic brands. Choose a brand that you find to be consistently good, with flavorful tomatoes and juice that isn't watery.

WATER

Unless you have good well water or exceptional tap water, use either filtered tap water or spring water for making broths, soups, and stews.

WINE

Many of the recipes in this book call for dry white wine, and some of them specify the type. For whites, I usually use an Italian varietal, such as Pinot Grigio, Soave, or Chardonnay, except in recipes that call for such fortified wines as sherry or Marsala. If you use a California white, stay away from the oaky Chardonnays and find a nice Sauvignon Blanc. For reds, a number of good sturdy wines can do the job, including Chianti or Montepulciano d'Abruzzo. In general, remember the old rule: don't cook with a wine you wouldn't drink.

RECIPES

Good homemade broth is easy to make and well worth the effort. It has a much richer, more genuine flavor than commercially prepared broth and will therefore yield a better-tasting soup or stew. However, commercial broth, either in cans, boxes, or dehydrated granules or cubes (bouillon), is often more convenient. When I don't have homemade broth on hand, I use a good-quality canned broth that is fat free and low in sodium. It works fine in many of the recipes in this book, and I have offered a choice of homemade or purchased in those recipes.

You must use homemade broth in some of the recipes, however, and these are indicated as well. Not surprisingly, they are mostly delicate, broth-based soups in which pasta or dumplings are cooked right in the broth. You can make the broth for these soups ahead of time and refrigerate it for up to 3 days or freeze it for up to 3 months.

Thoroughly wash all of your ingredients under cold running water for broth—meat, bones, scraps, vegetables, herbs—before putting them into a tall, narrow stockpot, and then cover them with fresh cold water (I use spring water). Let the broth simmer gently, skimming any foam that forms on the surface with a skimmer. Wait until the broth is almost done before adding salt. As broth cooks, it reduces in volume, intensifying the flavors. Adding salt too early can result in a broth that is too salty.

Strain the broth through a colander or sieve lined with a double layer of cheesecloth that has been rinsed in cold water and wrung out. Let the broth cool to room temperature before refrigerating it. Once it is chilled, you can remove the congealed layer of fat on the surface before reheating it.

Homemade Chicken Broth

BRODO DI POLLO

- 1 chicken, 4 to 4½ pounds, or 5 pounds chicken parts, including backs, necks, wings, and 1 chicken half

- 2 yellow onions, quartered, and 2 quarters each stuck with 1 whole clove

- 2 carrots, trimmed, halved lengthwise, and cut into 2-inch pieces

- 2 ribs celery, including leafy tops, trimmed and cut into 2-inch pieces

  Stalks from 1 fennel bulb (reserve bulb for another use)

- 6 sprigs fresh flat-leaf parsley

- 4 sprigs fresh thyme

- 1 clove garlic, lightly crushed with the flat side of a knife blade

- ½ teaspoon black peppercorns

- 4 to 5 quarts water

  Kosher or sea salt

COOK'S NOTE:

If you have used chicken parts and a half chicken, you can discard the solids. But if you have used a whole chicken, remove the meat from the bones, discarding the bones, skin, and any pieces of cartilage or other unattractive bits. You can serve the chicken, together with some of the carrots and pieces of celery, drizzled with good olive oil and sprinkled with salt and pepper. It makes a delicious light supper. Or, you can add some of the diced cooked chicken and vegetables to a bowl of pastina or rice cooked in the broth.

This broth is at once delicate and full bodied, and it fills the whole house with its comforting aroma as it cooks. I especially like the sweetness that the fennel stalks contribute. Several recipes in this book make use of this broth, including Crespelle in Brodo (page 98) and Cappelletti in Brodo per Natale (page 69).

MAKES 8 TO 10 CUPS (2 TO 2½ QUARTS)

Put all of the ingredients except the water and salt into a large stockpot. Add the water, pouring in enough to cover the ingredients by about 2 inches. Bring the broth to a boil over medium-high heat, skimming any foam that forms on the surface with a skimmer. Reduce the heat to medium-low and simmer gently, uncovered, skimming any foam that forms on the surface during the first hour or so of cooking, for 3 to 4 hours, adding salt to taste during the last hour of cooking. The broth is ready when it is reduced by about one-half and has developed a rich, meaty flavor.

Strain the broth through a colander lined with damp cheesecloth into a clean container (see Cook's Note for what to do with the solids). Let cool to room temperature, then cover and refrigerate until well chilled. Skim off and discard the congealed layer of fat on the surface before reheating. Use the broth within 3 days or freeze.

Rich Roasted Beef Broth

SOSTANZIOSO BRODO DI MANZO

2½ pounds boneless stewing beef such as chuck, cut into 3-inch pieces

2½ pounds beef marrowbones

3 carrots, peeled, halved lengthwise, and cut into 3-inch pieces

3 ribs celery, trimmed and cut into 3-inch pieces

8 fresh baby bella or cremini mushrooms, cleaned, stem ends trimmed, and cut in half

2 large yellow onions, quartered, each quarter stuck with 1 whole clove

2 tablespoons extra-virgin olive oil

½ teaspoon black peppercorns, lightly crushed

6 small sprigs fresh thyme

5 quarts water

Kosher or sea salt

COOK'S NOTE:
Resourceful Italians often serve the meat and vegetables, drizzled with good olive oil and sprinkled with salt and pepper, as a light second course to a broth-based soup.

Roasting the beef bones and vegetables gives this broth an exceptionally rich, robust flavor.

MAKES ABOUT 8 CUPS (2 QUARTS)

Heat the oven to 450 degrees F. Arrange the beef, marrowbones, carrots, celery, mushrooms, and onions in a large roasting pan. Drizzle the olive oil over the meat and vegetables and toss everything gently with a wooden spoon to coat with the oil. Roast, stirring once or twice, for about 45 minutes, or until the meat and bones are well browned.

Using tongs, transfer the beef, bones, and vegetables to a large stockpot. Then tip in the juices from the roasting pan. Add the peppercorns and thyme (you can tie them up in cheesecloth for easy retrieval, but I usually skip this step and let them float freely), and pour in the water. Bring to a boil over medium-high heat, skimming any foam that forms on the surface with a skimmer. Reduce the heat to medium or medium-low and simmer very gently, uncovered, skimming the surface as necessary for the first hour or so, for 5 hours, adding salt to taste during the last hour of cooking. The broth is done when it is reduced by about one-half and has developed a rich, meaty flavor.

Strain the broth through a colander lined with cheesecloth into a clean container. Discard the bones, and discard the meat and vegetables or reserve for another use (see Cook's Note). Let cool to room temperature, then cover and refrigerate until well chilled. Skim off and discard the congealed layer of fat on the surface before reheating. Use the broth within 3 days or freeze.

Homemade Meat Broth

BRODO DI CARNE

1 chicken, about 3½ pounds

4 beef marrowbones, 1½ to 1⅔ pounds total weight

3 carrots, peeled, halved lengthwise, and cut into 2-inch pieces

3 ribs celery, trimmed and cut into 2-inch pieces

2 yellow onions, quartered, each quarter stuck with 1 whole clove

1 teaspoon black peppercorns

6 sprigs fresh flat-leaf parsley, including stems, coarsely chopped (1 cup lightly packed)

5 quarts water

Kosher or sea salt

This versatile broth is a shade lighter in flavor than the Sostanzioso Brodo di Manzo (page 25) and is slightly more robust than Brodo di Pollo (page 24), which makes it perfect for many of the recipes in this book, including Minestra di Ceci e di Castagne (page 47), Zuppa di Grissini (page 41), and Zuppa al Vino Bianco (page 73).

MAKES ABOUT 10 CUPS (2½ QUARTS)

Put all of the ingredients except the salt in a large stockpot. Bring the broth to a boil over medium-high heat, skimming any foam that forms on the surface with a skimmer. Reduce the heat to medium-low and simmer gently, uncovered, skimming any foam that forms on the surface during the first hour or so of cooking, for 3 to 4 hours, adding salt to taste during the last hour of cooking. The broth is done when it is reduced by about one-half and has developed a rich, meaty flavor.

Strain the broth through a colander lined with damp cheesecloth into a clean container and discard the bones. See the Cook's Note on page 24 for a suggestion on how to serve the cooked chicken and vegetables. Let cool to room temperature, then cover and refrigerate until well chilled. Skim off and discard the congealed layer of fat on the surface before reheating. Use the broth within 3 days or freeze.

BRODO DI MAGRO

2 tablespoons extra-virgin olive oil

2 carrots, peeled, trimmed, and cut into 2-inch pieces

2 ribs celery, trimmed and cut into 2-inch pieces

1 large yellow onion, quartered, 2 quarters each stuck with 1 whole clove

1 leek, white and light green parts only, washed, trimmed, and cut into 1-inch pieces

Stalks and feathery leaves from 1 fennel bulb (reserve bulb for another use)

2 cloves garlic, lightly crushed with the flat side of a knife blade

5 or 6 sprigs fresh flat-leaf parsley, including stems, coarsely chopped (1 cup lightly packed)

2 sprigs fresh marjoram

2 sprigs fresh thyme

½ teaspoon black peppercorns

½ cup dry white wine

8 cups water

1 teaspoon kosher or sea salt

A splash of white wine gives this light vegetable broth a little extra body.

MAKES 6 TO 7 CUPS

In a Dutch oven or other heavy-bottomed pot, heat the olive oil over medium heat. Add all the vegetables, garlic, herbs, and peppercorns and sauté, stirring from time to time, for 10 to 15 minutes, or until the vegetables have softened and the onion is pale gold. Raise the heat to medium-high, pour in the wine, and let it simmer for 2 to 3 minutes. Add the water and salt and bring to a boil. Reduce the heat to medium-low and simmer gently, uncovered, for 45 minutes. The broth is done when it has reduced slightly and has a full flavor. Taste and adjust the seasoning with salt.

Strain the broth through a fine-mesh sieve lined with damp cheesecloth into a clean container. Use the back of a wooden spoon to press down on the solids, extracting as much liquid as possible. Discard the solids. Let the broth cool to room temperature, then cover and refrigerate for up to 3 days or freeze.

Fresh Tomato Sauce

SALSA FRESCA DI POMODORO

2 large cloves garlic, lightly crushed with the flat side of a knife blade

3 tablespoons extra-virgin olive oil

2½ to 2¾ pounds plum tomatoes (about 16), peeled, cored, seeded, and coarsely chopped (page 16)

1 teaspoon kosher or sea salt

5 fresh basil leaves, shredded or torn (about ¼ cup, lightly packed)

In summer, I like to make sauce from fresh, meaty, perfectly ripe plum tomatoes. Peeling and seeding tomatoes is not as much of a chore as you might think, and is certainly worth the effort.

MAKES 2½ TO 3 CUPS

In a large nonreactive saucepan, warm the garlic in the olive oil over medium heat. Use a wooden spoon to press down on the garlic to release its flavor and then swirl the pan to infuse the oil. After about 2 minutes, when the garlic begins to sizzle but before it starts to brown, carefully pour in the tomatoes (the oil can spatter) and stir to coat with the oil. Season with the salt, raise the heat to medium-high, and bring the tomatoes to a simmer. When the juices start bubbling, reduce the heat to medium-low and let the tomatoes simmer uncovered, stirring from time to time, for 25 to 30 minutes, or until thickened to a nice sauce consistency.

Remove from the heat and stir in the basil. Taste and adjust the seasoning with salt. Use immediately, or let cool to room temperature and store in the refrigerator for up to 3 days or in the freezer for up to 3 months.

Basic Tomato Sauce

SALSA SEMPLICE DI POMODORO

1 can (28 ounces) whole tomatoes

1 can (14½ ounces) stewed tomatoes

3 tablespoons extra-virgin olive oil

2 cloves garlic, lightly crushed with the flat side of a knife blade

½ teaspoon kosher or sea salt

10 fresh basil leaves, shredded or torn (about ½ cup)

When summer's tomatoes are gone, I use good-quality canned whole tomatoes, packed in their natural juices, to make sauce. I use canned stewed tomatoes here, too, to give the sauce a little extra zest. Be sure to look for stewed tomatoes without added spices.

MAKES 3¼ TO 3½ CUPS

Pour the whole tomatoes and their juice and the stewed tomatoes into a large bowl, and break them up with a potato masher or with your hands. Set aside.

In a large nonreactive saucepan, warm the oil and garlic over medium heat. Use a wooden spoon to press down on the garlic to release its flavor and then swirl the pan to infuse the oil. After about 2 minutes, when the garlic starts to sizzle and release its fragrance but before it starts to brown, carefully pour in the tomatoes (the oil can spatter) and stir to coat with the oil. Season with the salt, raise the heat to medium-high, and bring the tomatoes to a simmer. When the juices start bubbling, reduce the heat to medium and let the tomatoes simmer, uncovered, stirring from time to time, for 30 to 35 minutes, or until the sauce has thickened and the oil has separated from the tomatoes. Reduce the heat to medium-low if it is simmering too fiercely.

Remove from the heat and stir in the basil. Taste and adjust the seasoning with salt. Use immediately, or let cool to room temperature and store in the refrigerator for up to 3 days or in the freezer for up to 3 months.

Fresh Egg Pasta Dough
PASTA ALL'UOVO

2 cups unbleached all-purpose flour

1 tablespoon semolina flour, plus more for dusting work surface and sprinkling on dough

½ teaspoon kosher or sea salt

Pinch of freshly grated nutmeg

3 extra-large eggs

2 tablespoons extra-virgin olive oil

Purists maintain that truly good, tender pasta dough cannot be made in a food processor, but I disagree. Once you make this dough, you'll see why. This recipe is easy to follow and works every time. In this book, it is used for making cappelletti (page 69) and pasta grattata (page 71), but it is an excellent recipe for whenever you need to make fresh egg pasta.

MAKES ABOUT 1 POUND

To mix the dough, put the all-purpose flour, 1 tablespoon semolina flour, salt, and nutmeg in the work bowl of a food processor fitted with the metal blade. Pulse briefly to combine the dry ingredients. Break the eggs into the work bowl and drizzle in the olive oil. Process the mixture until the dough starts to form crumbs that look like small curds. This should take 20 seconds or less. Pinch together some of the mixture and roll it around. It should form a soft ball. If it seems dry, add a few drops of water—no more than a tablespoon—and process briefly.

Turn the mixture out onto a clean work surface and press it together with your hands to form a rough ball. Knead the dough, using the palm of your hand to push it gently but firmly away from you and then fold it over toward you. Give the dough a quarter-turn and continue to knead and turn for several minutes until the dough is smooth. Form it into a ball, wrap it tightly in plastic wrap, and let it rest at room temperature for 20 to 30 minutes.

To stretch the dough, first set up your pasta machine with the rollers on the widest setting (number 1 on my machine). Scatter a little semolina flour on the work surface around the machine and have more on hand for sprinkling on the dough.

Cut the dough into 3 equal portions and rewrap 2 portions. Knead the third portion briefly on the work surface. Then, using a rolling pin, roll it into an oval 5 to 6 inches long and about 3 to 4 inches wide. Feed the dough through the rollers of the pasta machine and lay the strip on your work surface. Fold the dough into thirds, like folding a business letter, sprinkle with a little semolina, and pass it through the rollers again.

CONTINUED

Repeat the folding and rolling process 4 more times, or until the strip of dough is smooth. Move the roller setting to the next notch and feed the strip of dough through the setting twice, sprinkling it with a little semolina to keep it from sticking each time and then moving the notch to the next setting. Continue passing the dough through the rollers of the pasta machine twice on each setting, until you get to setting 6 (or the narrowest setting on your machine). Roll the dough through the machine once with the notch on setting 6.

At this point you will have a long, thin ribbon of dough that can be cut and filled for *cappelletti*, or cut into noodles or other shapes for other recipes. Carefully lay the dough strip flat on a work surface dusted with semolina flour. For *cappelletti*, it is best to cut, fill, and shape the first ribbon of dough according to the recipe instructions (page 69) before stretching the next portion of dough. This will prevent the ribbons of dough from drying out too much.

CHAPTER 2

AUTUNNO
Recipes for Fall

39 Gnocchi di Semolina
in Brodo di Carne
Semolina Gnocchi in
Homemade Meat Broth

41 Zuppa di Grissini
Bread Stick Soup

42 Crema di Castagne
Cream of Chestnut Soup

43 Crema di Porcini
Creamy Porcini Soup

46 Zuppa di Lenticchie
Lentil Soup

47 Minestra di Ceci e di
Castagne
Chickpea and Chestnut Soup

49 Zuppa di Magro alla
Campagnola
Country Vegetable Soup

52 Fagioli Stufati con
Finocchio e Radicchio
Cranberry Bean Stew with
Fennel and Radicchio

53 Zuppa di Frutti di Mare
al Farouk
Curried Shellfish Stew

55 Pollo in Salsa Piccante
Chicken in Piquant Tomato Sauce

56 Spezzatino di Agnello con
Fagiolini e Farro
Lamb and Green Bean Stew
with Farro

57 Spezzatino di Maiale al
Sapore di Finocchio
Fennel-Scented Pork Stew

58 La Genovese
Neapolitan Braised Beef
with Onions

61 Rapini e Cavolo Riccio
Brasati
Braised Rapini and Kale

63 Cipolline Glassate
Glazed Onions in Cream

For all its Mediterranean splendor, Italy can be a chilly place in the fall. The long, hot days of August and September inevitably give way to cool October evenings and rainy days in November. Cold early morning mists blanket hilltops from Tuscany to the Marches. In cities, locals and tourists alike retreat from the afternoon drizzle by ducking into cafés for a quick shot of espresso or a thick hot chocolate.

But in the Italian kitchen things are just starting to heat up, with rich meat broths, thick *ragù*, and hearty bean and vegetable soups that warm body and spirit. My mother has many happy memories of autumns spent in Chieti, the hilltop city in Abruzzo where she grew up. During the harvest season, she would bundle up and walk from her house to her family's farm on the outskirts of town, where she spent countless hours watching the farmers' wives as they cooked around a gargantuan stone fireplace. There were more than a dozen women and they started before dawn, baking large *pizzelle* (thin, crispy waffles), which they slathered with black grape jam. The cooking continued all day. Newly butchered hogs were turned into sweet sausages to be eaten that day and salami and prosciutto to be cured over the next several months. There was homemade broth and thick cranberry bean soup, and simmering pots of duck *ragù* and pork rib stew.

My kitchen in Virginia (suburban Washington, DC, really) couldn't be farther removed from that pre–World War II farmhouse kitchen. But I am still inspired by my mother's reminiscences, and I often find myself thinking about them when I'm deciding what to make for dinner on a crisp fall evening. There is one stall at my local farmers' market that I can count on for fresh cranberry beans, at least for a couple of weeks, before their brief season has come and gone. Easier to come by are bunches of hardy greens—rapini, green and purple kale—to be added to soups or enjoyed on their own, with plenty of savory juice for sopping up with good bread. Now is the time for chestnuts and chickpeas and lentils. And even though mushrooms are available year-round at the supermarket, fall is when I crave them the most.

4 tablespoons unsalted butter, plus more for greasing the baking dish

3 extra-large eggs

1 cup freshly grated *Parmigiano-Reggiano* cheese, plus more for serving

⅔ cup semolina flour

½ teaspoon kosher or sea salt

Pinch of freshly grated nutmeg

6 cups *Brodo di Carne* (page 26)

COOK'S NOTE:
The semolina gnocchi can be baked ahead of time, cut into cubes, stored in a zipper-lock plastic bag or airtight lidded container, and refrigerated for up to 3 days or frozen for up to 1 month. If frozen, defrost gnocchi for about 1 hour and add them to the hot broth, giving them a little extra time to heat through.

Semolina Gnocchi in Homemade Meat Broth

GNOCCHI DI SEMOLINA IN BRODO DI CARNE

This old-fashioned soup, based on a recipe by legendary nineteenth-century Italian cookbook author Pellegrino Artusi, is a favorite in our house, especially in the fall. The hot broth and gentle flavors of the nutmeg-and-cheese-infused gnocchi will warm you right up after an afternoon spent on the soccer field or raking leaves in the yard. The cubes of semolina soak up the broth like tiny sponges.

MAKES 6 FIRST-COURSE SERVINGS OR 3 TO 4 MAIN-COURSE SERVINGS

Heat the oven to 325 degrees F. Generously butter a 9-inch round or square metal cake pan or glass baking dish.

In a small saucepan, melt the 4 tablespoons butter over low heat. Remove the pan from the heat as soon as the butter has melted.

In a bowl, whisk together the eggs and 1 cup cheese. Gradually whisk in the semolina, taking care to avoid lumps, and then the melted butter. Season with the salt and nutmeg.

Pour the semolina mixture into the prepared pan. Cover with aluminum foil and bake for 25 to 30 minutes, or until the semolina is set but not browned. Remove from the oven and let cool in the pan on a rack for 5 to 10 minutes. Run a knife around the inside edge of the pan to loosen the cake. Invert the pan and remove the cake. Set the cake on the rack, right side up, and let cool until tepid.

Cut the semolina cake into ¼-inch-thick slices, and cut the slices into ¼-inch cubes. You should have about 3 cups.

In a saucepot or saucepan large enough to accommodate the semolina gnocchi, bring the broth to a boil over medium-high heat. Carefully pour the semolina cubes into the broth, reduce the heat to medium-low, and simmer gently for 5 minutes, or until the gnocchi are heated through.

Ladle the soup into shallow bowls and sprinkle each serving with a little cheese.

Bread Stick Soup

ZUPPA DI GRISSINI

Extra-virgin olive oil for preparing pot

24 Piedmontese-style bread sticks (see Cook's Note)

4 ounces *toma piemontese* or similar semisoft cow's milk cheese such as Fontina or imported Muenster (see Cook's Note), thinly sliced or broken into small pieces

¼ teaspoon best-quality ground cinnamon

1 tablespoon unsalted butter, cut into small pieces

4 cups *Brodo di Carne* (page 26) or *Brodo di Pollo* (page 24), heated to a simmer

Freshly grated *Parmigiano-Reggiano* cheese for serving

COOK'S NOTE:

The bread sticks from Italy's Piedmont region are nothing like the tasteless, machine-made ones that bring to mind a 1970s-era Italian American restaurant. Rolled by hand into long, skinny ropes and baked in a hot oven, they are instead the bread sticks that you are likely to find on better restaurant tables across Italy. These classic *grissini* are increasingly available in the United States, packaged in long, rectangular boxes in the international section of your supermarket and at upscale grocery stores or Italian delicatessens.

Toma piemontese, a semisoft cheese made from unpasteurized cow's milk, has a mild and nutty flavor with a subtle tang. If you are unable to find it, you can substitute a similar French cheese called *tomme des Pyrénées*, Italian Fontina, or even a good imported Muenster from France or Germany.

Versions of this appealing antique soup can be found from western Piedmont into Valle d'Aosta, Italy's smallest and most mountainous region, which shares a border with France and Switzerland. In traditional households, a tureen of this cinnamon-laced soup, accompanied by a glass of wine and a lit candle, is set out on the dinner table on October 31, the night before All Saints' Day, in remembrance of the dead. You might expect bread sticks immersed in broth to become soft and spongy. But if you use the long, thin hand-rolled ones known as grissini piemontese, they puff up a bit and become satisfyingly chewy, like fat noodles.

MAKES 6 FIRST-COURSE SERVINGS OR 3 TO 4 MAIN-COURSE SERVINGS

Lightly coat the bottom of a Dutch oven or other heavy-bottomed pot with a lid with olive oil. Break the bread sticks in half. Arrange half of them on the bottom of the prepared pot. Sprinkle half of the toma and half of the cinnamon over the bread sticks and dot with half of the butter. Repeat with the remaining bread sticks, toma, cinnamon, and butter. Ladle the hot broth over the top.

Cover and simmer the soup over very low heat for 45 to 50 minutes, or until the bread sticks are soft but still retain their shape.

Ladle the soup into shallow bowls and sprinkle each serving with a little *Parmigiano-Reggiano* cheese.

Cream of Chestnut Soup

CREMA DI CASTAGNE

2 tablespoons unsalted butter

1 rib celery, trimmed and coarsely chopped

1 small yellow onion, coarsely chopped

1 pound (2 cups) peeled and cooked chestnuts, coarsely chopped

¼ cup plus 2 tablespoons dry Marsala

Kosher or sea salt

Freshly ground black pepper

4 cups *Brodo di Pollo* (page 24) or best-quality canned low-sodium chicken broth

½ cup heavy cream

1½ ounces pancetta, cut into ¼-inch dice

Whole-wheat croutons (see *Dadini di Pane al Pepe* variation, page 150) for serving

Chestnuts are plentiful in many parts of Italy, including Abruzzo, Tuscany, Piedmont, and the Alto Adige. Here in the United States, grocery stores usually stock them between Thanksgiving and New Year's Day. I have to admit, though, that the only time I buy whole, unpeeled chestnuts is when I want to roast them for eating plain. For most other recipes, including this one, I take the easy way out and buy cooked and peeled whole chestnuts. This soup is easy, elegant, and on the rich side. I would gladly give up dessert for a bowl of it.

MAKES 4 FIRST-COURSE SERVINGS

In a Dutch oven or other heavy-bottomed pot with a lid, melt the butter over medium heat. Add the celery and onion and sauté for 5 to 7 minutes, or until the onion is shiny and has begun to soften. Stir in the chestnuts, coating them well in the butter. Raise the heat to medium-high and pour in the ¼ cup Marsala. Stir and simmer for 2 minutes, or until some of the wine has evaporated.

Season with a little salt and pepper and reduce the heat to medium-low. Pour in the broth, cover partially, and cook for 20 minutes, or until the celery and onion are soft. Remove from the heat and let cool for 10 minutes.

In a blender, and working in 2 batches if necessary, purée the soup until completely smooth. Rinse out the pot and return the soup to it. Stir in the cream and the remaining 2 tablespoons Marsala. Bring the soup to a simmer over low heat, but do not let it boil.

While the soup is heating, put the pancetta in a small skillet, place over medium-high heat, and sauté for about 5 minutes, or until lightly crisped.

Taste the soup and adjust the seasoning with salt and pepper. Ladle the soup into shallow bowls and garnish with a sprinkle of the pancetta and a scattering of croutons.

Creamy Porcini Soup
CREMA DI PORCINI

1 ounce (1 cup) dried porcini mushrooms

1 cup boiling water

2 tablespoons extra-virgin olive oil

2 tablespoons unsalted butter

1 large clove garlic, minced

1 large yellow onion, chopped (about 2 cups)

8 ounces fresh white button mushrooms, cleaned, stem ends trimmed, and thinly sliced

8 ounces fresh baby bella or cremini mushrooms, cleaned, stem ends trimmed, and thinly sliced

¾ cup dry white wine or sherry

3 tablespoons all-purpose flour

5 cups *Brodo di Pollo* (page 24), *Brodo di Carne* (page 26), or best-quality canned low-sodium chicken broth

Kosher or sea salt

Freshly ground black pepper

12 ounces fresh large portobello mushrooms (about 3 large), cleaned, stems discarded, and caps thinly sliced

4 ounces fresh shiitake mushrooms, cleaned, stems discarded, and caps thinly sliced

½ cup heavy cream, at room temperature

2 tablespoons Cognac

¼ cup chopped fresh flat-leaf parsley

Whole-wheat croutons (see *Dadini di Pane al Pepe* variation, page 150) for serving

In a perfect world—at least in my perfect world—fresh porcini mushrooms, known for their meaty texture and distinct, earthy flavor, would be as common in the United States as they are in Umbria, Tuscany, and other parts of Italy in the fall. There, it is not unusual to see cars parked precariously along narrow mountain roads, temporarily abandoned by their owners who are off in search of the prized mushrooms. For this recipe, I've substituted a handful of dried porcini and a mix of other readily available fresh mushrooms, including portobellos and shiitakes.

MAKES 6 FIRST-COURSE SERVINGS OR 4 MAIN-COURSE SERVINGS

Put the porcini in a small heatproof bowl and pour the boiling water over them. Let soak for 20 to 30 minutes, or until softened. Drain the porcini in a fine-mesh sieve lined with damp paper towels or cheesecloth, reserving the liquid. Chop the mushrooms coarsely and set the mushrooms and liquid aside separately.

In a Dutch oven or other heavy-bottomed pot, heat 1 tablespoon each of the olive oil and butter over medium heat. Add the garlic and onion and sauté for about 5 minutes, or until the onion has softened and is translucent. Add the button mushrooms and baby bellas and sauté for 10 to 12 minutes, or until most of the liquid the mushrooms release has evaporated and they are tender. Stir in the porcini mushrooms, raise the heat to medium-high, and pour in the wine. Cook, stirring, for another 5 minutes or so, or until the wine has evaporated. Remove from the heat and let cool for 5 minutes.

In a blender, purée the cooked mushrooms together with the reserved porcini liquid until you have a smooth, creamy paste.

Return the purée to the pot and place over low heat. Sprinkle the flour over the purée and stir vigorously. Continue to stir as you gradually add the broth. When all the broth has been added, season to taste with salt and pepper, raise the heat to medium-low, and heat until the soup is hot but not simmering.

CONTINUED

Put the remaining 1 tablespoon each oil and butter in a large skillet over medium heat. Add the portobello and shiitake mushrooms and sauté, stirring frequently, for about 10 minutes, or until the liquid they release has evaporated.

Add the sautéed mushrooms to the soup. Slowly whisk in the cream and, finally, the Cognac, stirring for a couple of minutes until thoroughly combined and some of the alcohol has cooked off.

Ladle the soup into shallow bowls and garnish with the parsley and croutons.

Lentil Soup

ZUPPA DI LENTICCHIE

4 tablespoons extra-virgin olive oil

4 cloves garlic, lightly crushed with the flat side of a knife blade

1 yellow onion, finely chopped

2 carrots, peeled and cut into small dice

1 rib celery, trimmed and cut into small dice

2 cups brown lentils, rinsed and drained

4 cups *Brodo di Pollo* (page 24) or best-quality canned low-sodium chicken broth

4 cups water

2 sprigs fresh thyme

1 fresh bay leaf

1 teaspoon kosher or sea salt

Freshly ground black pepper

Dadini di Pane al Pepe (Black Pepper Croutons, page 150) for serving

COOK'S NOTE:
For an even heartier soup, add a small smoked pork chop to the pot while sautéing the vegetables. Remove the pork chop when the soup is cooked and, if you like, shred the meat and return it to the pot.

Never mind the military-drab color of this soup. The lentils give it a full, earthy flavor, which is enhanced by the herbs and the generous amount of garlic. It's just the thing to eat on a chilly fall day, especially when it is topped with a handful of pepper-spiced croutons.

MAKES 4 MAIN-COURSE SERVINGS

In a large Dutch oven or other heavy-bottomed pot, warm the olive oil over medium heat. Add the garlic, onion, carrots, and celery and sauté for 5 to 7 minutes, or until the onion is softened and pale gold and the carrots are bright orange. Stir in the lentils and sauté for a minute or two, mixing well to coat the lentils thoroughly with the oil and vegetables. Pour in the broth and water, and then add the thyme, bay leaf, salt, and several grinds of pepper. Cover partially and simmer, stirring from time to time, for about 45 minutes, or until the lentils are completely tender. Reduce the heat, if necessary, to keep the soup at a gentle simmer.

Discard the bay leaf. Taste and adjust the seasoning with salt. Spoon into deep bowls and garnish each serving with a handful of croutons.

Chickpea and Chestnut Soup

MINESTRA DI CECI E DI CASTAGNE

2 cups dried chickpeas, soaked overnight in water to cover

1 yellow onion, quartered

2 large cloves garlic, lightly crushed with the flat side of a knife blade

1 sprig fresh sage, plus 10 fresh sage leaves, finely chopped

5 tablespoons extra-virgin olive oil

Kosher or sea salt

3 cups *Brodo di Carne* (page 26), heated to a simmer

4 ounces thinly sliced *prosciutto di Parma*, cut crosswise into narrow ribbons

1 cup (8 ounces) peeled and cooked chestnuts, coarsely chopped

Freshly ground black pepper

Best-quality extra-virgin olive oil for serving

Crostoni al Pecorino (page 149) for serving

COOK'S NOTE:

This soup does not freeze well, but you can store it in the refrigerator for up to 3 days.

Chickpeas and chestnuts are an unusual—yet somehow natural—combination that turns up in the mountain cooking of Abruzzo. Both ingredients have a coarse texture that can be puréed to velvety smoothness, and both have a subtle earthy flavor that is brought to life when paired with an assertive, woodsy herb. And although rosemary is the traditional choice for this soup, I like the less typical choice of sage. This rustic soup shines when made with homemade broth and finished with a drizzle of a top-notch extra-virgin olive oil.

MAKES 4 TO 6 MAIN-COURSE SERVINGS

Drain the chickpeas and put them in a large Dutch oven or other heavy-bottomed pot. Add the onion, garlic, sage sprig, a generous drizzle—2 to 3 tablespoons—of olive oil, and water to cover by ¾ to 1 inch (about 8 cups).

Bring the chickpeas to a boil over medium-high heat, taking care to skim off any foam that appears on the surface with a skimmer. Reduce the heat to medium-low or low, as needed to maintain a gentle simmer, and cook, uncovered, for about 2 hours, or until the chickpeas are tender. Add salt to taste during the last 15 minutes of cooking—not too much, as you will be adding prosciutto to the soup later.

When the chickpeas are done, remove and discard the onion, garlic, and sage sprig. Let the chickpeas cool for 10 minutes. In a blender, working in batches, purée half of the chickpeas, along with some of the cooking liquid and 2 cups of the broth. Use a potato masher to coarsely mash the chickpeas remaining in the pot, leaving a few of them whole so that you have a mix of textures. Return the puréed chickpeas to the pot and reheat the soup on low heat.

Meanwhile, in a skillet, warm 2 tablespoons olive oil over medium heat. Stir in the chopped sage and the prosciutto and sauté for 2 minutes, or until the mixture is fragrant. Add the chestnuts and 2 small ladlefuls of the broth (½ to ¾ cup total) to the skillet and simmer for 2 to 3 minutes to allow the chestnuts to absorb some of the broth. You should have a coarse mash of chestnuts, prosciutto, and sage.

CONTINUED

Stir the chestnuts into the chickpeas and add the remaining broth
if the soup seems too thick (it should be somewhat thick, but not thick
enough to eat with a fork). Bring the soup to a simmer and cook
for 10 minutes. Taste and season with additional salt if needed and with
pepper to taste.

Ladle the soup into shallow bowls and garnish each serving with a
generous drizzle of your best olive oil. Do not skip this step, as it is crucial
to rounding out the soup's flavor. Serve topped with the *crostoni*.

Country Vegetable Soup

ZUPPA DI MAGRO ALLA CAMPAGNOLA

FOR THE BEANS

2 cups dried white beans such as *cannellini*, soaked overnight in water to cover

1 yellow onion, quartered

1 clove garlic, lightly crushed with the flat side of a knife blade

3 sprigs fresh flat-leaf parsley

6 cups water

Kosher or sea salt

FOR THE SOUP

3 tablespoons extra-virgin olive oil

1 yellow onion, finely chopped

1 rib celery, trimmed and finely chopped

2 cloves garlic, minced

2 carrots, peeled and sliced crosswise on the diagonal (1 cup)

2 yellow-fleshed potatoes such as Yukon gold, peeled and cut into ½-inch dice (1⅔ cups)

½ head green cabbage, about 8 ounces, shredded

8 ounces dinosaur kale, washed, trimmed, and shredded (see Cook's Note)

4 ounces beet greens, washed and shredded

1 cup canned whole tomatoes, passed through a food mill fitted with the plate with medium-sized holes

Kosher or sea salt

Freshly ground black pepper

FOR THE *RIBOLLITA*

6 large slices Italian country bread, each ½ inch thick

1 to 2 tablespoons extra-virgin olive oil

Best-quality extra-virgin olive oil for serving

This Tuscan specialty is two soups in one, a colorful, chunky vegetable soup and, when reheated with bread added to the mix, a classic peasant dish known as la ribollita. You can make it either way, or you can have it both ways: enjoy it as a vegetable soup one night, and add bread to the leftovers before reheating the following day. Just be sure to use less bread than the recipe calls for if you've already eaten some of the soup.

MAKES 6 MAIN-COURSE SERVINGS VEGETABLE SOUP OR 8 TO 10 MAIN-COURSE SERVINGS *RIBOLLITA*

TO MAKE THE BEANS:

Drain the beans and put them in a large saucepot or saucepan. Add the onion, garlic, parsley sprigs, and water. Bring to a boil over medium-high heat, taking care to skim off any foam that forms on the surface with a skimmer. Reduce the heat to medium-low or low, as needed to maintain a gentle simmer, and cook, uncovered, for about 2 hours, or until the beans are tender. Add salt to taste during the last 15 minutes of cooking. Remove from the heat and let cool for 10 minutes.

Remove and discard the onion, garlic, and parsley sprigs. In a blender, purée half of the beans along with some of the cooking liquid. Reserve both the puréed and whole beans.

TO MAKE THE SOUP:

In a large Dutch oven or other heavy-bottomed pot with a lid, heat the olive oil over medium heat. Add the onion, celery, and garlic and sauté, stirring, for 7 to 8 minutes, or until the vegetables have begun to soften. Add the carrots, potatoes, cabbage, kale, and beet greens and stir to combine thoroughly. Stir in the puréed tomatoes and season with salt and pepper. Reduce the heat to medium-low, cover, and simmer for 10 minutes, or until the greens have begun to wilt and soften.

Add the whole and puréed beans along with any remaining cooking liquid. Cover and simmer over low heat, stirring occasionally, for 45 minutes to 1 hour, or until the vegetables are completely tender and the soup has thickened. Add additional water (up to 3 cups) if the soup seems too thick.

CONTINUED

COOK'S NOTE:
Dinosaur kale, also known as *cavolo nero*, *lacinato* kale, and Tuscan black cabbage, is a mild-flavored cabbage with long, slim, crinkly, dark blue-green leaves. It has become easier to find than in the past, and is available at many farmers' markets, well-stocked supermarkets, and gourmet grocery stores. Use regular green curly-leaf kale if you are unable to find dinosaur kale.

At this point, the soup can be eaten as is, or cooled, covered, and stored in the refrigerator for up to 3 days.

TO MAKE THE *RIBOLLITA*:
Heat the oven to 375 degrees F. Arrange the bread slices on a rimmed baking sheet and place in the oven for 15 to 20 minutes, or until lightly toasted. Remove from the oven and let cool.

In a large Dutch oven or other heavy-bottomed pot, heat 1 to 2 tablespoons olive oil over medium heat. Tear up 2 slices of the toasted bread and place them in the bottom of the pot. Ladle one-third of the soup over the bread. Repeat with 2 more slices of bread and half of the remaining soup. Add a final layer of bread and top with the remaining soup. Reduce the heat to medium-low or low, as needed to maintain a gentle simmer, and simmer, stirring gently from time to time, until the soup begins to bubble and is thoroughly heated through. As the soup is cooking, taste and add more salt if necessary.

Ladle the *ribollita* into shallow bowls and drizzle each serving with your best olive oil.

FAGIOLI STUFATI CON FINOCCHIO E RADICCHIO

- 1 pound shelled fresh cranberry or *borlotti* beans (about 2 pounds in the pod)

- 2 small sprigs fresh oregano

- 2 small sprigs fresh rosemary

- 2 small sprigs fresh sage

- 4 cloves garlic, lightly crushed with the flat side of a knife blade

- 3 or 4 tablespoons extra-virgin olive oil

  Kosher or sea salt

- 2 slices hickory-smoked or apple wood–smoked bacon, 3 ounces total weight, cut crosswise into ½-inch-wide strips

- 1 small or ½ medium fennel bulb, trimmed, cut into wedges, and wedges thinly sliced crosswise

- ½ head radicchio, shredded (about 1¼ cups)

- 1 can (14 ounces) whole tomatoes, seeded and coarsely chopped

- 2 small dried chili peppers or generous pinch of red pepper flakes

- ½ red onion, sliced paper-thin

  Best-quality extra-virgin olive oil for serving

COOK'S NOTE:

This stew is practically a meal in itself, but I like to serve it with some sliced *ricotta salata*, a dense, fresh sheep's milk cheese that has been salted and pressed. *Ricotta salata* can be sliced or crumbled and is good to eat out of hand, as part of an antipasto platter, or tossed into salad or on cooked pasta. It also makes an excellent side dish for steak or roasted chicken.

In Virginia, where I live, cranberry beans—similar to Italian borlotti beans— are also known as October beans, and they are available as shelling beans—fresh in their pods—for a few weeks in early fall. Although I have occasionally seen them at well-stocked supermarkets, you are more likely to come across them at a farmers' market. I love how the dark, streaky red and creamy white of the beans are echoed in the smoky bacon, red onion, and radicchio of the recipe. As it cooks, the radicchio loses its characteristic bitterness and takes on a soft, nutty flavor.

MAKES 3 TO 4 MAIN-COURSE SERVINGS OR 6 SIDE-DISH SERVINGS

In a medium Dutch oven or other heavy-bottomed pot with a lid, combine the beans with water to cover by 1 inch. Add 1 sprig each of the oregano, rosemary, and sage, 2 of the garlic cloves, and 2 tablespoons olive oil. Cover, place over medium-high heat, and bring to a boil. Reduce the heat to medium-low, cover partially, and simmer for 30 minutes, or until the beans are tender but still hold their shape. Add salt to taste during the last 10 minutes of cooking.

While the beans are cooking, finely chop the remaining sprigs of oregano, rosemary, and sage and set aside. Put the bacon in a large Dutch oven or other heavy-bottomed pot over medium-high heat and cook for about 5 minutes, or until it has rendered some of its fat and is slightly crisp. If there is not much fat in the pan, add 1 or 2 tablespoons olive oil and then stir the remaining garlic, chopped herbs, fennel, and radicchio into the bacon. Reduce the heat to medium and sauté briefly until the radicchio has wilted. Add the tomatoes and chili peppers and simmer for 10 minutes, or until the mixture is slightly thickened. Turn off the heat until the beans are done cooking.

When the beans are tender, discard the herb sprigs and garlic. Add the beans and their liquid to the pot with the sauce and cook over medium heat for about 10 minutes to give the beans a chance to absorb some of the flavors of the sauce. Stir in the onion and then taste and adjust with salt if needed. Remove from the heat.

Ladle the stew into shallow bowls and drizzle each serving with a little of your best olive oil.

Curried Shellfish Stew

ZUPPA DI FRUTTI DI MARE AL FAROUK

1 tablespoon extra-virgin olive oil

1 tablespoon unsalted butter

1 large or 2 medium yellow onions, chopped (about 2 cups)

3 quarter-sized pieces fresh ginger

2 sprigs fresh thyme

1 fresh bay leaf

1 tablespoon curry powder

Large pinch of saffron threads diluted in the juice of ½ lemon

Freshly ground black pepper

1½ cups dry white wine

1½ cups light cream

24 littleneck clams or other small clams, thoroughly cleaned (page 16)

24 mussels, thoroughly cleaned (page 16)

16 jumbo shrimp, peeled and deveined (page 16)

½ teaspoon kosher or sea salt

COOK'S NOTE:
The shellfish can be cleaned several hours in advance and stored in the refrigerator.

When I was growing up, I spent most of my summers at the beach, in the once-sleepy fishing village of Silvi Marina (now a tourist-clogged resort) on the Adriatic coast. One of my family's favorite restaurants was in the nearby port city of Pescara. It was a casual place right on the beach, specializing in seafood. Among the signature dishes was spaghetti al Farouk, which featured local shellfish in a beguiling curry-flavored sauce named after the Egyptian king who fled to Italy in 1952, after being deposed. My mother re-created the sauce in her kitchen, and later I adapted it further and came up with this fragrant stew. Serve with chunks of crusty Italian or multigrain bread on the side.

MAKES 4 MAIN-COURSE SERVINGS

In a large Dutch oven or other heavy-bottomed pot with a lid, heat the olive oil and butter over medium heat. Add the onions and sauté for 6 to 8 minutes, or until they have softened and are translucent. Stir in the ginger, thyme, bay leaf, curry powder, and diluted saffron and season with a little pepper. Pour in the wine, raise the heat to medium-high, bring to a steady simmer, and simmer for 3 minutes.

While the broth is simmering, pour the cream into a small saucepan and warm slightly over gentle heat. Do not let it boil.

Place a bowl large enough to hold all the shellfish near the stove. Tip the clams into the simmering broth, cover, and cook for about 3 minutes, or until about half of them have opened. Add the mussels, stirring to coat them with the broth, cover, and cook for 2 to 3 minutes, or until they begin to open. Add the shrimp, stirring to combine them with all the shellfish, cover, and simmer for about 5 minutes, or until the shrimp are just cooked through. Using a slotted spoon, remove the shellfish to the bowl and cover to keep warm. Discard any clams or mussels that failed to open.

Remove the pot of broth from the heat. Line a fine-mesh sieve with damp cheesecloth and place it over a saucepan. Strain the broth into the saucepan, discarding the solids. Stir the warm cream into the broth. Season with the salt; taste and add more salt—the amount will depend on how salty the liquor from the clams and mussels is. Place over medium heat and bring the broth just to a simmer, taking care not to let it boil.

Divide the clams, mussels, and shrimp among 4 shallow bowls. Pour the broth over the shellfish, dividing it evenly, and serve.

Chicken in Piquant Tomato Sauce

POLLO IN SALSA PICCANTE

2 tablespoons extra-virgin olive oil

10 chicken thighs

Kosher or sea salt

Freshly ground black pepper

1 large or 2 medium yellow onions, chopped (about 2½ cups)

1 clove garlic, finely minced

1 to 2 tablespoons all-purpose flour

¾ cup dry white wine

4 Rizzoli brand *alici in salsa piccante* (page 18) or best-quality Italian anchovy fillets in olive oil, drained and chopped

Generous pinch of red pepper flakes

1 can (28 ounces) whole tomatoes, coarsely crushed with a potato masher or fork

COOK'S NOTE:
I may be in the minority, but I have never liked chicken skin. So, once it has done its job of rendering some pan drippings and flavor during the initial browning, I prefer to remove it. (If left to simmer in the sauce, it will lose its crispness and turn flabby, and make the sauce unnecessarily fatty. Where's the appeal in that?)

Meaty chicken thighs are simmered to tender succulence in a lush, spicy sauce of onions, tomatoes, and anchovies. Why thighs? Because they have lots of flavor and can stand up to long simmering without losing moisture. As for the anchovies, I won't even try to make a plea in their defense; I don't believe they need one. They are a staple in southern Italian cooking and I wouldn't think of making this dish without them. They add an essential layer of flavor. This is delicious served over rice, pasta, or polenta, but I like polenta (page 154) best for soaking up the sauce.

MAKES 5 TO 6 MAIN-COURSE SERVINGS

Heat the oven to 350 degrees F.

In a large Dutch oven or other heavy-bottomed pot, heat the olive oil over medium heat. When the oil is hot, place half the chicken thighs, skin side down, in the pot and sprinkle with salt and pepper. Cook the chicken for about 5 minutes, or until the skin side is browned and crisp. Using tongs, turn the chicken thighs over. Sprinkle with a little more salt and pepper and let brown for about 5 minutes longer. Using the tongs, remove the thighs to a deep plate and repeat with the remaining thighs, removing them to the plate when they are browned.

If the chicken has rendered a lot of fat, pour off all but about 2 tablespoons. Return the pot to medium heat, add the onion, and cook for about 5 minutes, or until just beginning to soften. Stir in the garlic and sauté for another minute or two, or until the garlic releases its fragrance. Sprinkle in the flour and mix well. Pour in the wine, stir to combine, and cook for 2 to 3 minutes, or until some of the liquid has evaporated. Add the anchovies and red pepper flakes and then add the tomatoes.

Using your fingers, peel the skin off the chicken thighs (see Cook's Note) and discard. Arrange the chicken pieces in the Dutch oven with the sauce, along with any juices that have accumulated in the plate. Cover the pot and put it in the oven. Cook for 30 minutes; uncover and cook for 1 hour longer, or until the sauce has thickened and the thighs are very tender.

Taste and adjust the seasoning with salt and pepper and then serve in individual bowls.

SPEZZATINO DI AGNELLO CON FAGIOLINI E FARRO

2 tablespoons extra-virgin olive oil

1½ pounds boneless lamb stew meat (leg or shoulder), cut into 1-inch cubes

2 yellow onions, chopped (about 2 cups)

3 cloves garlic, lightly crushed with the flat side of a knife blade

½ cup dry red wine

2 cups *Brodo di Pollo* (page 24) or best-quality canned low-sodium chicken broth

1 can (14 ounces) whole tomatoes, coarsely crushed with a potato masher or fork

½ cup *Salsa Semplice di Pomodoro* (page 30) or best-quality commercial tomato sauce

¾ cup *farro*, rinsed and drained

1 pound green beans, stem ends trimmed and snapped in half (about 4 cups)

1 teaspoon kosher or sea salt

Freshly ground black pepper

1 fresh bay leaf

10 large fresh basil leaves, cut crosswise into fine strips (chiffonade)

COOK'S NOTE:
Farro is available at Italian food markets, gourmet markets, and some supermarkets and by mail order (see Sources, page 163). Wheat berries, a close relative, can be substituted.

This is my Italianized version of my friend Michelle Andonian's Armenian lamb stew with green beans, a dish she has served many times to grateful friends in her Detroit photography studio. Here, I've added farro, an ancient grain closely related to the wheat berry that has made a comeback in Italian kitchens in the past decade. If you have a vegetable garden, this is the perfect opportunity to use up any mature pole or bush beans that are still hanging around. Like the meat, the beans become fork-tender during simmering, absorbing the savory juices of the stew.

MAKES 4 MAIN-COURSE SERVINGS

In a large Dutch oven or other heavy-bottomed pot with a lid, warm the olive oil over medium-high heat. When the oil is hot, arrange the lamb cubes on the bottom of the pot and sear, turning as needed, for 8 to 10 minutes, or until browned on all sides. Add the onions and garlic, reduce the heat to medium, and sauté for 5 to 7 minutes, or until the onions are pale gold. Pour in the wine and let it boil, stirring, for 5 minutes or so, or until it has almost evaporated. Stir in the broth, crushed tomatoes, tomato sauce, *farro*, green beans, salt, and several grinds of pepper, then add the bay leaf. Bring the stew to a boil, reduce heat to medium-low, cover, and simmer gently for 1½ to 2 hours, or until the lamb is fork-tender and the *farro* is tender; most of the liquid will have been absorbed.

Discard the bay leaf. Ladle the stew into shallow bowls and top each serving with a sprinkle of basil.

Fennel-Scented Pork Stew

SPEZZATINO DI MAIALE AL SAPORE DI FINOCCHIO

2 to 4 tablespoons extra-virgin olive oil

2 pounds boneless pork loin (top or center cut) or pork shoulder, cut into 1-inch cubes

Kosher or sea salt

Freshly ground black pepper

1 carrot, peeled and finely chopped

1 rib celery, trimmed and finely chopped

1 small yellow onion, finely chopped

1 small fennel bulb, trimmed and finely chopped

Generous pinch of red pepper flakes

2 cloves garlic, passed through a garlic press

1 teaspoon finely minced fresh rosemary

2 teaspoons crushed fennel seeds (see Cook's Note)

¾ cup dry white wine

2 cups canned whole tomatoes, passed through a food mill fitted with the plate with medium-sized holes

COOK'S NOTE:

To crush the fennel seeds, put them in a zipper-lock plastic bag and pound them gently but firmly with a meat pounder, heavy rolling pin, or bottom of a cast-iron skillet, or other similarly heavy object.

As good as this stew is on its own, it is even better served over a steaming bowl of polenta (page 154).

The town of Deruta, in southern Umbria, has been famous for centuries for its hand-painted majolica ceramics. Along the highway leading to town, warehouses and factories crammed with everything from giant tabletops and planters to decorative spoon rests lure tourists from around the globe. Inside the town's stone walls, the narrow streets are lined with shops displaying their best wares: intricately designed long-necked vessels, gracefully curved urns, and plates painted with pastoral landscapes. After my family and I spent a chilly morning window-shopping in a fine-mist drizzle, we were directed by one of the shop owners to a cheerful restaurant with a heated, glass-enclosed terrace and bright ceramic-topped tables. We warmed up with a delicious stew of wild boar robustly flavored with fennel and rosemary. When we returned home from our trip, I cooked up this variation in my kitchen. You can make it either with pork loin or pork shoulder. Pork loin will yield a stew that is less fatty but not quite as tender as one made with shoulder meat.

MAKES 4 MAIN-COURSE SERVINGS

In a large Dutch oven or other heavy-bottomed pot, heat 2 tablespoons olive oil over medium to medium-high heat. When the oil is hot, arrange about one-fourth of the pork cubes on the bottom of the pot and sprinkle with a little salt and pepper. Sear the pork, turning the pieces every few minutes, until they are more or less colored on all sides. Using a slotted spoon, remove to a deep plate or bowl. Continue to brown the pork in batches, adding additional oil if necessary.

After you have removed the last batch of pork, add 1 tablespoon oil to the pot if there are not enough pan drippings to sauté the vegetables. Add the carrot, celery, onion, fennel bulb, and red pepper flakes to the pot and reduce the heat to medium-low. Cook the vegetables, stirring frequently, for 8 to 10 minutes, or until they are slightly softened and shiny.

In a small bowl, mix together the garlic, rosemary, fennel seeds, and ½ teaspoon salt to form a paste. Add the paste to the vegetables and stir for 1 minute. Raise the heat to medium-high and pour in the wine. Stir well and let the liquid boil for 2 minutes or so, or until some of the wine has evaporated. Return the pork to the pot. Stir in the tomato purée, bring to a boil, reduce the heat to low, cover, and simmer for 1 hour. Uncover and simmer for 30 more minutes, or until the meat is very tender and the sauce is thick.

Ladle the stew into shallow bowls and serve.

Neapolitan Braised Beef with Onions
LA GENOVESE

1 boneless chuck roast, 2 pounds, tied

Kosher or sea salt

Freshly ground black pepper

2 tablespoons extra-virgin olive oil

1 carrot, peeled and finely chopped

1 large rib celery, trimmed and finely chopped

1½ ounces pancetta, minced

1 teaspoon finely chopped fresh marjoram

1 teaspoon finely chopped fresh thyme

4 pounds yellow onions, halved and sliced paper-thin

1 cup dry white wine

1 pound dried short, sturdy pasta such as penne or *ziti*

Freshly grated *Parmigiano-Reggiano* or *pecorino romano* cheese for serving

When I was a child, I traveled with my family to visit friends in the town of Caserta, outside of Naples. I was only eleven or twelve, but I can still remember the lunch that the hostess, Nunzia Venditti, prepared: pasta with a creamy, robustly flavored onion sauce. I had never had anything like it before. It wasn't until much later that I learned that this alluring, tomato-free sauce was—despite its northern Italian name—a Neapolitan specialty. This is a two-course dish, with the sauce dressing pasta for the first course and spooned over beef slices for the second course. Serve a salad of red leaf lettuce and radicchio alongside the beef.

MAKES 6 FIRST-COURSE SERVINGS WITH PASTA AND 6 SECOND-COURSE MEAT SERVINGS

Season the chuck roast with a little salt and pepper. In a Dutch oven or other heavy-bottomed pot with a lid, heat the olive oil over medium heat. When the oil is hot, put the meat in the pot and sear for 4 to 5 minutes on each side, or until well browned on all sides. Remove the meat to a plate.

Add the carrot, celery, pancetta, marjoram, and thyme to the pot and sauté, stirring, for 5 minutes, or until the vegetables are shiny and the pancetta is somewhat browned. Return the meat to the pot and add the onions, arranging them over the meat. Cover and simmer for about 20 minutes, or until the onions have started to wilt and release their juices. Reduce the heat to low, and let the meat and vegetables simmer gently, covered, for 40 minutes.

Uncover, turn the meat, re-cover, and continue to cook, turning the meat again every 30 minutes, for 2 hours. This will bring the total cooking time to 3 hours. At this point the meat should be very tender. Remove it to a plate or bowl and cover with aluminum foil to keep it warm.

Raise the heat to medium and stir ¼ cup of the wine into the onions. Continue to cook and stir for 3 to 5 minutes, or until the wine has evaporated and the onions begin to adhere to the bottom of the pot. Continue to add the wine in this way, ¼ cup at a time, until you have used it all and the onion sauce is brown and creamy.

58

Cook the pasta in a large pot of boiling water generously seasoned with salt. When the pasta is al dente (the cooking time will vary depending on which pasta you use and the brand), drain it in a colander placed in the sink and then return it to the pot. Dress the pasta with some of the onion sauce, mixing it gently but thoroughly to make sure it is well coated.

Serve the pasta in individual bowls with lots of freshly grated cheese for a *primo piatto* (first course). Slice the meat and serve it as a second course with a little sauce spooned over the slices (or reheat the meat and serve with the sauce the following day).

Braised Rapini and Kale

RAPINI E CAVOLO RICCIO BRASATI

2 bunches rapini (2½ pounds before cleaning)

2 bunches kale (1¼ pounds before cleaning)

7 cloves garlic, halved

Kosher or sea salt

¾ to 1 cup extra-virgin olive oil

1 to 1½ cups dry white wine

2 dried chili peppers, crumbled, or generous pinch of red pepper flakes

This is my Italian version of southern "pot likker" greens, pungent and garlicky and full of bold flavor. I used to make it only with rapini (also known as broccoli di rape and broccoli rabe, a strong-tasting, somewhat bitter leafy green with small florets). A few years ago I decided to add kale to the mix and was immediately addicted. While kale is also a sturdy green, it adds a complementary sweet note to the peppery pungency of the rapini. I know it says that this recipe serves six as a side dish, but left to my own devices I could pretty easily consume a whole pot of it by myself. Fortunately, or perhaps unfortunately, my husband loves these braised greens as much as I do. They go great with pork chops, roast chicken, or lamb. But you can also chop them coarsely once they're cooked, stir in a little butter, and toss them with cooked pasta.

MAKES 6 SIDE-DISH SERVINGS

Wash and trim the greens, cutting or snapping off the tough bottoms of the stems, but leaving the more tender part. Tear any large leaves of kale or rapini crosswise into 2 or 3 pieces.

Put a couple of large handfuls of the greens, with the washing water still clinging to them, into a large, high-sided saucepan or kettle and place over medium-high heat. Strew a few pieces of the garlic over the greens and then pour over about ⅓ cup of the olive oil and ½ cup of the wine. Sprinkle with a little salt and bits of chili. Cover the pot and let the greens cook for 5 to 7 minutes, or until they have begun to wilt and there is room in the pot to add more. Reduce the heat to medium and add another couple of handfuls of greens, along with more garlic, oil, wine, salt, and chili. Cover the pot and cook for another 5 to 7 minutes, or until the greens have wilted. Use a long, two-pronged serving fork or tongs to mix the greens well, and then add any remaining greens along with a drizzle more of oil, a splash of wine, and any remaining garlic and chili. Cover and braise for 30 to 40 minutes, stirring with the fork from time to time. The greens are done when they have become very dark and tender.

Transfer the greens to a decorative ceramic bowl to serve.

Glazed Onions in Cream

CIPOLLINE GLASSATE

2 pounds *cipolline* or small white boiling onions, 1½ inches in diameter (about 20) (see Cook's Note)

2 tablespoons unsalted butter

½ to 1 teaspoon kosher or sea salt

Freshly ground black pepper

¼ cup heavy cream, at room temperature

½ teaspoon chopped fresh sage

½ teaspoon chopped fresh thyme

COOK'S NOTE:

Cipolline are an Italian variety of pearl onions, recognizable by their squat, saucerlike shape. They are available in many well-stocked supermarkets and farmers' markets.

The sweet, squat Italian onions known as cipolline take on a beautiful glassy sheen and silky texture as they simmer slowly in a rich sauce. This dish is full of the aromas and flavors of fall and pairs well with just about any kind of roast, whether chicken, lamb, pork, or veal. It is a must-have at my Thanksgiving table.

MAKES 4 TO 6 SIDE-DISH SERVINGS

Bring a large saucepan filled with water to a boil. Peel the onions and then blanch them in the water for 1 minute. Drain thoroughly.

In a wide, deep-sided sauté pan, melt the butter over medium-low heat. Place the onions in the pan in a single layer. Turn them to coat with the butter. Pour over enough water just to cover the onions barely (larger onions may not be completely covered). Season with the salt and pepper. Raise the heat to medium and cook the onions uncovered, gently stirring them from time to time, for about 1 hour, or until nearly all the water has evaporated, leaving a small amount of syrupy glaze.

Reduce the heat to medium-low. Pour the cream over the onions and sprinkle on the sage and thyme. Cook the onions, turning them to coat with the liquid, for a couple of minutes longer, or until the cream has thickened to a sauce.

Spoon the onions and sauce into a ceramic serving bowl or decorative covered dish to serve at the table.

CHAPTER 3

INVERNO

Recipes for Winter

69 Cappelletti in Brodo
    per Natale
    Stuffed Pasta "Hats" in Broth for
    Christmas

71 Minestra di Pasta Grattata
    Grated Pasta Soup

72 Canederli in Brodo
    Dumplings in Broth

73 Zuppa al Vino Bianco
    White Wine Soup

74 Zuppa di Cipolle al
    Pecorino
    Onion Soup with Pecorino

76 Pasta e Patate alla Paprica
    Pasta and Potato Soup
    with Paprika

77 Pasta e Fagioli Invernale
    Pasta and Bean Soup with
    Christmas Limas

79 Calamari in Umido per la
    Vigilia di Natale
    Christmas Eve Calamari

80 Zuppa di Pesce allo
    Zafferano
    Saffron-Scented Fish Stew

83 Pollo Stufato con Trebbiano
    Whole Chicken Stewed in
    Trebbiano

85 Salsicce e Lenticchie
    all'Umbriana
    Sausages and Lentils in the
    Style of Umbria

86 Costate di Maiale in Salsa di
    Pomodoro e Porcini
    Pork Ribs in Tomato-Porcini
    Sauce

88 Osso Buco in Salsa Bruna
    Braised Veal Shanks in Brown
    Sauce

90 Spezzatino al Ginepro
    Beef Stew with Juniper Berries

92 Indivia Brasata al Forno
    Oven-Braised Endive

In December, cooking at my house revolves around cooking for the holidays. If I've got my act together (not always the case), I've turned the carcass of the Thanksgiving turkey—or in my case, capon—into a fragrant broth and stored it in the freezer for Christmas Day. And either my mother or I have also made and frozen the *cappelletti*, the stuffed pasta "hats" to be cooked in the broth (okay—it's usually her).

Deciding on the menu for Christmas Eve is the easiest task. With a few minor changes, it is the same reassuring mix of seafood and braised vegetable dishes that has graced the table for decades, starting with my mother's *capellini* (angel hair pasta) in tuna *ragù* and ending with a large assortment of cookies, lovingly and obsessively prepared by my mother, my sister, and me. The star of the show, however, is always the *calamari*, stewed to tenderness in a rich red sauce.

The end of the holidays does not mean the end of winter. One hardly has to make the case for a good, hearty soup or stew in January and February; the comfort factor is undeniable. A whole stewed chicken, thick country-style onion soup, beef stew scented with juniper berries—take your pick. Or, if you're looking for a way to chase away the midwinter blues, you might think about throwing a buffet-style soup and stew party. Offer meat and vegetarian choices, along with some fresh country bread, and set out stacks of colorful, mismatched bowls for your guests to help themselves.

Stuffed Pasta "Hats" in Broth for Christmas

CAPPELLETTI IN BRODO PER NATALE

FOR THE *CAPPELLETTI* STUFFING

- 1 tablespoon extra-virgin olive oil
- 1 tablespoon unsalted butter
- 5 ounces ground chicken breast
- 5 ounces ground pork
- 5 ounces ground veal
- 1 small yellow onion, finely chopped
- 1 clove garlic, sliced paper-thin
- 1 teaspoon kosher or sea salt, or to taste

  Freshly ground black pepper
- ½ cup dry white wine
- 2 large eggs
- ½ cup freshly grated *Parmigiano-Reggiano* cheese
- 2 ounces *prosciutto di Parma*, finely julienned
- 2 ounces mortadella, finely chopped

  Pinch of freshly grated nutmeg

FOR THE *CAPPELLETTI*

  Semolina flour for dusting work surface
- 1 batch *Pasta all'Uovo* (page 31)

  Cappelletti stuffing

FOR THE SOUP

- 10 cups (2½ quarts) *Brodo di Pollo* (page 24)

  Freshly grated *Parmigiano-Reggiano* cheese for serving

This is my family's traditional first course on Christmas Day, as it is for many Italian families. It is by far the most challenging recipe in the book because it calls for making stuffed pasta and broth. But please do not be deterred. What's great about this recipe is that you can make it in steps and you do most of the work ahead of time. Both the cappelletti, once formed, and the broth can be frozen. When the time comes to serve this most delicious soup, just heat the broth in a pot until it is boiling and drop in the pasta—straight from the freezer.

MAKES 120 *CAPPELLETTI*, TO SERVE 6 TO 8 AS A FIRST COURSE

TO MAKE THE STUFFING:

In a sauté pan, heat the olive oil and butter over medium heat. When the butter has melted and begins to sizzle, add the chicken, pork, veal, onion, and garlic. Use a wooden spoon to break up the large chunks of meat. Sauté, stirring, for 2 minutes, then cover and let the meat cook for 12 to 15 minutes, or until the onion is soft and the meat is cooked through but not browned. Season the mixture with the salt and pepper to taste. Raise the heat to medium-high and pour in the wine. Cook for 2 more minutes, or until most of the liquid has evaporated. Remove from the heat and let cool for 10 minutes.

Transfer the stuffing to a food processor and process for 10 to 15 seconds, or until it is finely ground but not a paste—you want the mixture to have some body. Transfer the mixture to a bowl.

In a small bowl, stir together the eggs and the cheese. Pour the egg mixture into the bowl with the meat. Add the prosciutto, mortadella, and nutmeg and mix everything together thoroughly. Cover tightly and refrigerate until ready to use.

TO MAKE THE *CAPPELLETTI*:

Cover a large space with a tablecloth and sprinkle the cloth with semolina. This is where you will put the *cappelletti* once you have shaped them.

Roll out the first piece of pasta dough as directed in the recipe. You should have a thin ribbon about 3 feet long. Cut the ribbon in half crosswise and lay both halves out on your work space. Cover 1 piece with plastic wrap while you cut and shape the other piece.

CONTINUED

Using a 2-inch round cookie cutter, cut out as many circles of dough as possible. You should get about 20 circles. Spoon a scant 1 teaspoon stuffing onto the center of each circle. Working with 1 circle at a time, wet the tip of your finger with water, run it around the edge of the circle, and fold the circle into a half-moon, pressing the edge to seal. When all of the half-moons are formed, pick up 1 half-moon and, using both hands, fold the top of the rounded side in toward you while bringing the corners together; slightly overlap the corners and pinch them together to seal. What you should have is a little round "bonnet" or "hat" enclosing the stuffing. With a toothpick or thin metal skewer, prick 3 holes in the center of the hat and then place the pasta on the semolina-sprinkled tablecloth. Continue to form *cappelletti* with the rest of the half-moons, transferring them to the tablecloth as they are shaped. Remove the plastic wrap from the other ribbon half; cut the dough into circles, stuff, and shape into *cappelletti* in the same manner. Continue to roll out and shape the remaining pasta dough until you have used it all. You should end up with 120 *cappelletti*. Return any unused stuffing to the refrigerator, or freeze for later use.

If you are serving the *cappelletti* the same day, leave them out on the tablecloth until you are ready to cook them in the broth, but no more than a couple of hours. Otherwise, place them on flat trays or rimmed baking sheets that have been sprinkled with semolina and put the trays in the freezer (as many as will fit at one time). Freeze the *cappelletti* for 15 to 30 minutes, or until firm. Transfer them to zipper-lock plastic freezer bags and freeze them for up to 3 months.

TO MAKE THE SOUP:

In a large saucepot, bring the broth to a boil over medium heat. Carefully lower the *cappelletti* into the boiling broth and raise the heat to medium-high to return the broth to a boil. Cook the *cappelletti* for about 5 minutes once the broth has returned to a boil. Carefully stir them from time to time with a wooden spoon to make sure they do not stick together. The only real way to know if the *cappelletti* are cooked is to taste one; the pasta should be tender but not soggy.

Ladle the *cappelletti* and broth into shallow bowls, counting out 15 to 20 *cappelletti* per serving. Sprinkle each serving with the cheese.

MINESTRA DI PASTA GRATTATA

1 batch *Pasta all'Uovo* (page 31)

Semolina flour for dusting work surface

8 cups (2 quarts) *Sostanzioso Brodo di Manzo* (page 25)

Freshly grated *Parmigiano-Reggiano* cheese for serving

A rich homemade beef broth is essential to the integrity of this soup, in which a rustic pasta is simmered in the broth and absorbs its deep beef flavor. Pasta grattata is a clever way to enjoy homemade pasta without a lot of work; you simply grate pieces of dough on the large holes of a box grater to create little shavings.

MAKES 6 TO 8 FIRST-COURSE SERVINGS

TO MAKE THE *PASTA GRATTATA*:

Mix and knead the pasta dough as directed in the recipe, but do not roll it out after it has rested. Instead, cut the dough into 8 equal portions and let it sit, uncovered, for about 15 minutes to dry out slightly.

Lightly sprinkle the work surface and several rimmed baking sheets or trays with semolina. Using the large holes of a box grater, grate the dough, 1 portion at a time. As the dough shavings accumulate, gently scoop them up or brush them onto the prepared baking sheets. Spread the shavings out in a single layer so they don't stick together in big clumps. Let them dry for 2 hours; if there are clumps, wait until the pasta has dried out a bit before gently separating them (don't worry about small clumps; they will cook fine). When the pasta has dried, carefully transfer it to a large sieve or colander, 1 tray at a time, and gently shake out any excess semolina. Return the pasta to the trays.

TO MAKE THE SOUP:

In a large saucepot, bring the broth to a boil over medium-high heat. Pour in the grated pasta, reduce the heat to medium, and simmer vigorously for 15 to 20 minutes, or until the pasta is tender.

Ladle the soup into shallow bowls and sprinkle each serving with the cheese.

Dumplings in Broth

CANEDERLI IN BRODO

8 cups lightly packed cubed, crust-free day-old Italian country bread

2 cups milk, heated to lukewarm

1 tablespoon unsalted butter

1 small yellow onion, finely chopped

2 large eggs, lightly beaten

2 tablespoons minced fresh flat-leaf parsley

2 ounces imported mortadella, cut into small (¼-inch) dice (½ cup)

1½ ounces (about 4 thin slices) Genoa salami, finely julienned (½ cup)

1 teaspoon kosher or sea salt

2 tablespoons buckwheat flour or all-purpose flour, plus more for coating

8 to 10 cups *Brodo di Carne* (page 26) or *Sostanzioso Brodo di Manzo* (page 25)

Freshly grated *Parmigiano-Reggiano* cheese for serving

COOK'S NOTE:
Some recipes call for cooking the dumplings in water and then adding them to the broth, presumably to avoid floating bits of dumpling should any fall apart. However, I much prefer to poach them in the broth so that they absorb its flavor. You can test your *canederli* mixture by making a small dumpling and poaching it in a little broth or salted water. If it falls apart, add more flour to the mixture before shaping the rest of the dumplings.

There is something undeniably alluring about these oversized dumplings. They are, in spite of their hefty appearance, surprisingly light and fluffy, thanks to gentle poaching in broth. Dig into one with your spoon and you are rewarded with savory bites of salami and mortadella. Traditional canederli are made with speck, a lightly smoked ham from Trentino–Alto Adige in northern Italy. I use mortadella instead because it is easier to find and I prefer its milder, nutty flavor. You can make a meatless version, too, with chopped blanched spinach or other greens and mushrooms taking the place of the ham. Either way, you should poach the dumplings in a rich homemade meat broth to give them their proper due.

MAKES 8 FIRST-COURSE OR 4 MAIN-COURSE SERVINGS

Put the bread in a large bowl and pour the milk over it. Stir with a wooden spoon or spatula and then let the mixture sit for 1 hour to allow the bread to absorb the milk.

In a small skillet, melt the butter over medium heat. Add the onion and sauté for 5 to 7 minutes, or until it has softened and is translucent. Remove from the heat and let cool slightly.

Add the cooked onion, eggs, parsley, mortadella, salami, and salt to the bread and stir until the ingredients are well combined. Sprinkle in the flour and work it in with a wooden spoon or spatula.

Divide the mixture into 8 equal portions. Wet your hands with cold water to keep the mixture from sticking to them. Shape each portion into a round dumpling slightly smaller than a tennis ball. Be sure to pack the mixture tightly as you make the dumplings; otherwise, they may fall apart while simmering in the broth (see Cook's Note). Spread the flour on a flat plate, then, one at a time, roll the dumplings in the flour, coating them lightly. As the dumplings are coated, put them on a platter. Let them rest for 10 to 20 minutes.

Meanwhile, select a pot large enough to keep the dumplings completely immersed as they cook. If you do not have a big enough pot, you can cook the dumplings in 2 batches. Pour in the broth and bring to a boil over medium-high heat. Carefully lower the dumplings, one at a time, into the boiling broth. Reduce the heat to medium-low or low, as needed to maintain a gentle simmer, and simmer for 15 to 18 minutes, or until they are cooked through.

With a large spoon, scoop out the dumplings and transfer them to a large serving tureen or to individual shallow bowls. Pour the hot broth over the dumplings. Sprinkle each serving with the cheese.

White Wine Soup

FOR THE CROUTONS

2 tablespoons unsalted butter

1 slice whole-wheat bread, with crust, cut into ¼-inch cubes

½ teaspoon ground cinnamon

FOR THE SOUP

3 cups *Brodo di Carne* (page 26)

1 cup dry white Italian wine, preferably Pinot Bianco, Pinot Grigio, or Chardonnay from Alto Adige

1 cup heavy cream, at room temperature

4 large egg yolks

1 rounded tablespoon all-purpose flour

This unusual soup has its origins in beautiful, mountainous Alto Adige, Italy's northernmost region, bordering Austria and Switzerland. The area is known for its high-quality dry white wines, and it is wine that gives this soup its distinctive sharp note and cuts the richness of the cream and egg yolks. Cinnamon-dusted croutons add both a rustic touch and a trace of the exotic. This is a perfect first course for an intimate midwinter dinner party.

MAKES 4 FIRST-COURSE SERVINGS

TO MAKE THE CROUTONS:

In a small skillet, melt the butter over medium heat. Put in the bread cubes and stir to coat. Sprinkle the cinnamon over the bread cubes and toss well. Sauté the bread cubes, tossing frequently, for about 5 minutes, or until browned and lightly crisped. Remove the croutons to a bowl and set aside.

TO MAKE THE SOUP:

In a Dutch oven or other heavy-bottomed pot, bring the broth to a boil over medium-high heat. Boil the broth until it is reduced by about one-third (to 2 cups). This should take about 15 minutes. Reduce the heat to medium and stir in the wine and then the heavy cream. Bring the mixture to a simmer, but do not let it boil. Reduce the heat to medium-low.

Temper the egg yolks before adding them to the soup: In a bowl, lightly beat the egg yolks just until blended. Stirring constantly, very slowly whisk about ¼ cup of the hot cream mixture—a splash at a time—into the yolks. Then, carefully whisk the egg yolk mixture back into the soup, stirring all the while. Continue to stir for about 5 minutes, or until the soup is creamy and slightly thickened. Put the flour into a small fine-mesh sieve and slowly sprinkle it over the soup, whisking as you go so that no lumps form. Continue to stir and cook the soup for 5 more minutes, or until it is about the consistency of heavy cream or just slightly thicker. It should barely coat the back of a wooden spoon but be thinner than custard.

Ladle the soup into 4 small bowls and sprinkle an equal amount of the croutons over each serving.

ZUPPA DI CIPOLLE AL PECORINO

4 tablespoons unsalted butter

3 pounds yellow onions or a mix of yellow and red, halved and thinly sliced

1 teaspoon minced fresh marjoram

1 teaspoon kosher or sea salt

¼ cup dry Marsala

1 tablespoon tomato paste

4 cups *Brodo di Pollo* (page 24), *Brodo di Carne* (page 26), *Brodo di Magro* (page 27), or best-quality canned low-sodium beef broth, heated to a simmer

8 *Crostini al Pepe* (see variation, page 148)

Freshly grated *pecorino romano* cheese for serving

Although onion soup is usually associated with French cuisine, Italians have countless renditions, each one as delicious as the next. The Tuscan version, called cipollata, is a thick stew of slow-cooked onions into which eggs are beaten at the last minute. Umbrians add a touch of tomato to theirs, and in Calabria, Marsala and a shot of grappa are used to flavor the soup. I've taken some liberties and combined my favorite elements from several versions to come up with this one.

MAKES 4 MAIN-COURSE SERVINGS

In a Dutch oven or other heavy-bottomed pot, melt the butter over medium heat. When the butter has melted and begins to sizzle, add the onions and stir to coat well. Sprinkle in the marjoram and salt, reduce the heat to low, and let the onions cook, uncovered, stirring from time to time, for 45 minutes, or until they are golden and velvety soft.

Raise the heat to medium-high and pour in the Marsala. Cook, stirring, for 2 minutes, or until some of the wine has evaporated. In a small bowl, stir together the tomato paste and ¼ cup of the broth. Add the diluted tomato paste to the soup and stir. Pour in the rest of the broth. Reduce the heat to low once again and simmer, partially covered, for 45 minutes.

Taste the soup and adjust the seasoning with salt. Place 2 *crostini* into each of 4 shallow bowls. Ladle the soup over the bread and sprinkle each serving with a tablespoon or two of cheese.

PASTA E PATATE ALLA PAPRICA

Except in areas of the north, paprika is not a common ingredient in Italian cooking. But I love it in this thick, rustic soup, where it imparts a smoky sweetness and a beautiful baked-clay color. To heighten the smoky flavor even more, I sometimes add a pinch of smoked Spanish paprika.

MAKES 4 TO 5 MAIN-COURSE SERVINGS

- 2 tablespoons extra-virgin olive oil
- 1 tablespoon finely minced fatback or pancetta
- 1 bunch scallions (about 6), ends trimmed and white and green parts thinly sliced crosswise
- 2 carrots, peeled, cut into ¼-inch-thick rounds, and rounds quartered
- 1½ pounds yellow-fleshed potatoes such as Yukon gold, peeled and cut into ½-inch dice
- ½ teaspoon kosher or sea salt
- ½ teaspoon sweet Hungarian paprika
- Generous pinch of ground cayenne pepper
- ½ cup canned whole tomatoes, passed through a food mill fitted with the plate with medium-sized holes
- 6 to 7 cups *Brodo di Pollo* (page 24) or best-quality canned low-sodium chicken broth
- 1½ cups small dried pasta such as shells or *ditalini*
- 1 cup freshly grated *pecorino romano* cheese
- 2 tablespoons minced fresh flat-leaf parsley

In a Dutch oven or other heavy-bottomed pot with a lid, heat the olive oil and fatback over medium heat. Add the scallions and carrots and sauté, stirring occasionally, for about 10 minutes, or until their colors are bright. Add the potatoes, salt, paprika, and cayenne and cook, stirring, for a minute or two, or until the potatoes are well coated. Stir in the tomato purée and 3 cups of the broth. Raise the heat to medium-high and bring to a boil. Reduce the heat to medium-low, cover, and cook at a gentle but steady simmer for 20 to 25 minutes, or until the potatoes and carrots are tender.

Add 3 more cups broth, raise the heat to medium-high, and bring the soup to a boil. Stir in the pasta and cook, uncovered, until the pasta is al dente; the cooking time will vary depending on which pasta shape you use and the brand and how thick the broth is. If the soup is too thick, or if you prefer it a little soupier, add some or all of the remaining 1 cup broth while the pasta is cooking.

Remove the soup from the heat and stir in ½ cup of the cheese and the parsley. Taste and adjust the seasoning with salt and paprika. Let the soup sit for just a minute or two before ladling it into a soup tureen or individual bowls. Sprinkle with the remaining cheese.

PASTA E FAGIOLI INVERNALE

2 cups dried Christmas limas, soaked overnight in water to cover

3 ounces pancetta, finely minced

1 small rib celery, trimmed and finely chopped

1 yellow onion, finely chopped

3 large cloves garlic, passed through a garlic press

1 tablespoon minced fresh rosemary

½ cup extra-virgin olive oil

8 cups water (2 quarts)

Kosher or sea salt

Generous pinch of red pepper flakes

8 ounces dried fettuccine or spaghetti, broken into 1-inch pieces

Best-quality extra-virgin olive oil for serving

Christmas limas are my favorite beans to cook in winter. They are dense and filling, and their taste reminds me of chestnuts. The beans are named for their appearance: Freshly shelled, they are the palest green, with streaks of red. As they dry, the pale green fades to cream and the red darkens. If you can't find Christmas limas locally, you can mail order them (see Sources, page 163), or you can use another large dried bean, such as borlotti or cranberry.

MAKES 8 MAIN-COURSE SERVINGS

Drain the beans and place them in a large Dutch oven or other heavy-bottomed pot with a lid and add the pancetta, celery, and onion. In a small bowl, mix together the garlic and rosemary to form a paste and add the paste to the pot. Drizzle in the ½ cup olive oil and stir to combine the contents of the pot thoroughly. Pour in the water and bring to a boil over medium-high heat. Reduce the heat to low, cover partially, and simmer for about 2 hours, or until the beans are very tender. Remove from the heat and let the soup cool for 15 minutes or so.

In a blender, purée half the soup until smooth and then return it to the pot and stir well. Season the soup to taste with salt, add the red pepper flakes, and then bring to a boil over medium-high heat. Don't worry if the soup seems a little watery at this point; it will thicken up nicely once you add the broken noodles.

Stir in the pasta and cook at a gentle simmer (reduce the heat to medium if necessary) for about 20 minutes, or until the pasta is al dente.

Ladle the soup into shallow bowls and drizzle each serving with your best olive oil.

Christmas Eve Calamari

CALAMARI IN UMIDO PER LA VIGILIA DI NATALE

2 pounds cleaned calamari, both sacs and tentacles, washed and thoroughly dried with paper towels (see Cook's Note)

3 tablespoons extra-virgin olive oil

1 large yellow onion, halved and thinly sliced

2 large cloves garlic, passed through a garlic press

½ teaspoon kosher or sea salt

Generous pinch of red pepper flakes

1 teaspoon finely chopped fresh oregano

¼ cup dry white wine

1 can (14½ ounces) stewed tomatoes

1 tablespoon red wine vinegar

1 tablespoon finely chopped fresh flat-leaf parsley

8 slices *Bruschetta* (page 151)

COOK'S NOTE:

Frozen calamari are available in 2½- to 3-pound blocks. To thaw, place the block in a large bowl of cold water for about 30 minutes, or until the individual pieces separate easily. Drain thoroughly and pat dry.

You can serve this calamari dish with *Risotto Semplice* (page 152) instead of *bruschetta*, but be sure to omit the cheese. My sister likes to use any leftover stew as a sauce for pasta.

This classic dish of calamari braised in tomato sauce has a special place in my heart. It has always been, and still is, the star attraction at my family's traditional Christmas Eve fish dinner. Back in the 1960s and 1970s, before squid were popular in the United States, my mother would order them ahead of time from her fish market. They were sold whole and not cleaned, so she would set about this messy and time-consuming task early in the morning on Christmas Eve day, separating the tentacles from the sacs, removing the thin bone inside the sac, and peeling off the gray outer skin. I'm embarrassed to say that my sister and I, who referred to calamari as creepy crawlers, never offered to help clean them, though we were always ready to devour them at the table. Now, thank goodness, it is easy to find cleaned calamari, both fresh and frozen (see Cook's Note). Either is fine for this recipe.

MAKES 4 MAIN-COURSE SERVINGS

With kitchen scissors, cut the calamari sacs into ½-inch-wide rings. Cut each crown of tentacles in half lengthwise to yield bite-sized pieces.

In a large sauté pan with a lid, heat the olive oil over medium heat. Add the onion and sauté, stirring from time to time, for 7 to 8 minutes, or until softened and translucent. In a small bowl, mix together the garlic and the salt to form a paste and add the paste to the onion. Add the red pepper flakes and oregano and stir to incorporate everything thoroughly. Stir in the calamari and sauté for a minute or two. Raise the heat to medium-high and add the wine. Let the mixture bubble for 2 minutes, and then pour in the tomatoes. Reduce the heat to medium-low, cover partially, and let cook for 30 minutes.

Uncover and continue to stew for an additional 15 minutes, or until the sauce has thickened. Stir in the vinegar, raise the heat to high, and cook for about 2 more minutes. Taste and adjust the seasoning with salt if needed. Remove from the heat and stir in the parsley. Serve in shallow bowls and accompany with the *bruschetta*.

ZUPPA DI PESCE ALLO ZAFFERANO

½ cup extra-virgin olive oil

5 cloves garlic, lightly crushed with the flat side of a knife

1 carrot, peeled and coarsely chopped

1 rib celery, trimmed and coarsely chopped

1 small yellow onion, coarsely chopped

1 cup coarsely chopped fresh flat-leaf parsley, stems included, plus 2 tablespoons finely minced, leaves only

2 small lobster tails, removed from their shells (see Cook's Note), cut into 2-inch chunks, and shells washed and reserved

16 large shrimp, peeled and deveined (see page 16), shells washed and reserved

1¾ cups dry white wine

4 cups water

Kosher or sea salt

Generous pinch of saffron threads (about ½ teaspoon)

¼ teaspoon red pepper flakes, or more to taste

2 cups canned whole tomatoes, drained and coarsely chopped or coarsely crushed with a potato masher or fork

2 pounds firm, meaty white fish fillets or steaks such as cod, hake, grouper, monkfish, or red snapper, cut into 2-inch chunks

18 littleneck or other small clams, thoroughly cleaned (see page 16)

18 mussels, thoroughly cleaned (see page 16)

6 or 12 slices *Bruschetta* (page 151)

There are as many recipes for fish stew as there are kitchens in Italy. Even Umbria, the country's only landlocked region, claims a version featuring the fish from picturesque Lake Trasimeno, surrounded by green hills dotted with medieval villages. Some variations specify shellfish only, while others call for a mix of fin and shellfish. Fish stews are easy to make, and they don't take much time since fish and shellfish cook so quickly. This version, which includes lobster tails, was suggested by my sister, Maria, an excellent cook. The lobster and shrimp shells are used to make a quick, fragrant stock. A pinch of saffron adds an alluring note and a golden tinge to the spicy tomato-based broth.

MAKES 6 MAIN-COURSE SERVINGS

TO MAKE THE SHELLFISH BROTH:
In a saucepan, heat ¼ cup of the olive oil over medium heat. Stir in 2 cloves of the garlic, the carrot, celery, and onion. Sauté for 5 minutes, or until the vegetables have softened. Add the coarsely chopped parsley and the lobster and shrimp shells. Cook for about 2 minutes, or until the shells start to change color. Increase the heat to medium-high and pour in 1 cup of the wine. Boil for about 2 minutes, or until some of the wine evaporates. Pour in the water, add about 1 teaspoon salt, and bring to a boil. Reduce the heat to medium and let the stock simmer for 30 to 40 minutes, or until sufficiently flavored. Taste for salt and adjust the seasoning.

Drain the stock through a fine-mesh sieve lined with damp cheesecloth placed over a bowl. Discard the solids and return the stock to the saucepan. You should have 2 to 2½ cups. Bring to a gentle boil over medium heat and reduce the stock further, to about 1½ cups. Cover the stock to keep it hot while you prepare the stew (reheat on low if necessary).

TO MAKE THE STEW:
Put the saffron threads in a small bowl and stir in 3 tablespoons of the hot broth. Let the mixture sit for 10 to 15 minutes, stirring once or twice, or until the saffron threads have dissolved.

To remove the lobster meat from a
tail shell, make a vertical cut through
the softer underside of the shell
from top to bottom and pry it open a
little bit to loosen the meat. Use your
fingers or a small fork to push the
meat from the bottom through the
top opening of the shell.

In a large Dutch oven or other heavy-bottomed pot with a lid, heat the remaining $\frac{1}{4}$ cup olive oil over medium heat. Add the remaining 3 garlic cloves and the red pepper flakes and sauté for a minute or two, or until the garlic releases its fragrance. Pour in the tomatoes, the remaining $\frac{3}{4}$ cup wine, the remaining reduced shellfish broth, and the diluted saffron. Bring the liquid to a boil and let it simmer for a couple of minutes to allow the flavors to mingle.

Add all of the seafood to the pot except for the mussels and the shrimp. Cover and let the stew simmer for 8 to 10 minutes, or until at least half the clams have opened and the fish is opaque. As it cooks, carefully stir once or twice and reduce the heat to medium-low if it is simmering too hard. Add the mussels and shrimp to the pot, re-cover, and cook for about 5 minutes, or until all the clams have opened, the mussels have opened, and the shrimp are cooked. Sprinkle on the minced parsley and stir to incorporate. Some of the more tender fin fish, such as hake, will have flaked apart, thickening the broth. Discard any clams or mussels that failed to open.

Place 1 or 2 slices of *bruschetta* in the bottom of each of 6 shallow bowls. Ladle the stew over the bread, making sure that each bowl contains a good mix of fish and shellfish.

Whole Chicken Stewed in Trebbiano

POLLO STUFATO CON TREBBIANO

1 ounce (1 cup) dried porcini mushrooms

1 cup boiling water

1 tablespoon unsalted butter

1 tablespoon extra-virgin olive oil

1 whole chicken, 3 pounds, rinsed and thoroughly dried and legs tied together with kitchen string

Kosher or sea salt

Freshly ground black pepper

1 large or 2 medium yellow onions, peeled and finely chopped (about 2 cups)

1 small carrot, peeled and finely chopped

2 ounces *prosciutto di Parma*, finely chopped

¾ cup Trebbiano d'Abruzzo

Risotto Semplice (page 152) for serving

Trebbiano is one of the world's most widely planted grapes. In Italy, it is used to produce a variety of wines, including Trebbiano d'Abruzzo, a crisp, straw-colored everyday white that pairs especially well with chicken. In this recipe, a whole chicken is stewed in a small amount of the wine, creating a delectable, full-bodied sauce.

MAKES 4 MAIN-COURSE SERVINGS

Put the porcini in a small heatproof bowl and pour the boiling water over them. Let soak for 20 to 30 minutes, or until softened. Drain the porcini in a fine-mesh sieve lined with damp paper towels or cheesecloth, reserving the liquid. Chop the mushrooms coarsely and set the mushrooms and liquid aside separately.

In a Dutch oven or other heavy-bottomed pot, heat the butter and olive oil over medium heat. When the butter has melted and starts to sizzle, add the chicken, breast side down, and sprinkle it with a little salt and pepper. Brown the chicken, giving it a quarter turn every 3 minutes, until it is golden brown all over. Carefully remove the chicken to a deep platter or large bowl (I use a long pair of tongs and a wide, sturdy metal spatula). Pour out all but 2 tablespoons of the fat. (If the butter is too brown by this point, pour out all the fat and discard, wipe out the bottom of the pot with paper towels, and heat 2 fresh tablespoons olive oil.)

Return the pot to medium heat and stir in the onion, carrot, prosciutto, and chopped porcini and sauté for 7 to 8 minutes, or until the onion has softened and is translucent. Raise the heat to high and stir in the wine and reserved porcini liquid. Let the liquid boil for about 4 minutes, or until some of it has evaporated. Reduce the heat to low and return the chicken to the pot, breast side down. Spoon some of the liquid over the chicken, cover, and let it stew gently for 30 minutes. Turn the chicken over so that it is breast side up, re-cover, and stew for another 30 to 45 minutes, or until the chicken is cooked through and the meat comes easily off the bone. Taste and adjust seasoning with salt and pepper if necessary.

Remove the chicken to a cutting board and cut it into 8 to 10 serving pieces. Arrange the pieces on a serving platter and spoon some of the sauce over them. Serve the chicken with the risotto, spooning a little of the sauce over the rice as well.

SALSICCE E LENTICCHIE ALL'UMBRIANA

1¾ cups brown lentils, rinsed and drained

3 cups water

2 cloves garlic, lightly crushed with the flat side of a knife blade

1 rib celery, trimmed and finely chopped except for a 1-inch piece

1 fresh bay leaf

1 teaspoon Kosher or sea salt

2 tablespoons extra-virgin olive oil

6 fresh sweet Italian sausages, halved crosswise to make 12 pieces

¼ cup finely chopped yellow onion

1 cup *Salsa Semplice di Pomodoro* (page 30) or best-quality commercial tomato sauce

2 cups *Brodo di Carne* (page 26) or best-quality canned low-sodium beef broth

Freshly ground black pepper

This is a classic stew from the hill towns of Umbria, where it is prepared with freshly made sweet sausages and tiny green-brown lentils from the fields of Castelluccio. The lentils are renowned throughout Italy and beyond for their delicate flavor and thin skins, which practically disappear during cooking while the legumes retain their shape and toothy texture. Lentils from Castelluccio, as well as other similar Italian lentils, are available at some Italian delicatessens and gourmet food stores and by mail order, but if you can't find them, use plain brown lentils. This is a perfect meal to make on a cold, windy day, when the last of the leaves are falling and you need a bowl of comfort.

MAKES 4 TO 6 MAIN-COURSE SERVINGS

Put the lentils in a heavy-bottomed saucepan and add the water, 1 of the garlic cloves, the 1-inch piece celery, the bay leaf, and the salt.

Bring the lentils to a boil over medium heat, reduce the heat to medium-low, cover partially, and simmer for about 30 minutes, or until just slightly undercooked. Remove from the heat and set aside.

In a heavy-bottomed Dutch oven, heat the olive oil over medium heat. When the oil is hot, add sausages and cook, turning them as needed, for 10 to 15 minutes, or until browned on all sides. Remove the sausages to a plate, leaving the fat in the pot.

Add the remaining garlic clove, the chopped celery, and the onion to the pot and sauté the vegetables for 7 to 8 minutes, or until they have softened and are pale gold but not browned. Pour in the tomato sauce, stir well, and then pour in the broth, again stirring to combine thoroughly. Return the sausages to the pot and add the lentils. Season the stew with freshly ground pepper. Reduce the heat to low and simmer, uncovered, for 30 minutes, or until the lentils are completely tender.

Discard the bay leaf. Serve the stew in shallow bowls.

Pork Ribs in Tomato-Porcini Sauce
COSTATE DI MAIALE IN SALSA DI POMODORO E PORCINI

½ ounce (½ cup) dried porcini mushrooms

1 cup boiling water

1½ to 1¾ pounds boneless country-style pork ribs, trimmed of excess exterior fat

2 tablespoons extra-virgin olive oil

Kosher or sea salt

Freshly ground black pepper

1 clove garlic, lightly crushed with the flat side of a knife blade

1 large or 2 medium yellow onions, finely chopped (about 2 cups)

2 carrots, peeled and finely chopped

1 rib celery, trimmed and finely chopped

1 cup *Salsa Semplice di Pomodoro* (page 30) or best-quality commercial tomato sauce

1 cup sturdy red wine such as a good Chianti or Zinfandel

1 fresh bay leaf

1 pound dried *pappardelle*, farfalle, or fettuccine

Freshly grated *Parmigiano-Reggiano* cheese for serving

I've come to think of this stew as a poor man's osso buco (page 88). Both stews feature rich, dark, unctuous sauces and succulent, fork-tender meat. But country-style pork ribs—thick-cut slabs with lots of meat—are a lot less expensive than veal shanks. Because this stew is so rich, I like to serve it as a sauce over pasta rather than on its own; the wide ribbons known as pappardelle are my first choice, although the sauce pairs just as well with farfalle or fettuccine. It is also good over polenta (page 154). This recipe will serve four people generously. You can shred the meat right into the sauce before you toss it with the cooked pasta, or place a few small chunks on top of the dressed pasta.

MAKES 4 TO 6 MAIN-COURSE SERVINGS

Heat the oven to 325 degrees F.

Put the porcini in a small heatproof bowl and pour the boiling water over them. Set aside to soak for 20 to 30 minutes.

In a large Dutch oven or other heavy-bottomed pot with a lid, heat the olive oil over medium heat. Cut the pork ribs in half crosswise and, when the oil is hot, put half of the ribs in the hot oil. Sprinkle them with a little salt and pepper and let them brown well without turning them for about 4 minutes. Turn and brown on the other side for 3 to 4 minutes, sprinkling with a little more salt and pepper. Remove the ribs to a shallow bowl or plate and repeat with the remaining ribs, salting and peppering them as you brown them.

When all the ribs have been browned, pour off all but about 2 tablespoons of the fat from the pot. Return the pot to medium heat and add the garlic, onion, carrots, and celery. Sauté the vegetables for 5 to 7 minutes, or until the onion has softened and is translucent.

Meanwhile, drain the porcini in a fine-mesh sieve lined with damp paper towels or cheesecloth, reserving the liquid, and chop the mushrooms finely. When the vegetables are ready, add the mushrooms, together with their liquid. Simmer for 5 minutes, and then add the tomato sauce, wine, and bay leaf. Return the ribs to the pot and bring the stew to a boil.

Cover and put the pot in the oven. Braise for 1¾ hours, or until the meat is fork-tender and the sauce is reduced to a rich, dark gravy. Taste and adjust seasoning with salt and pepper if necessary.

Cook the pasta in a large pot of boiling water generously seasoned with salt. When the pasta is al dente (the cooking time will vary depending on which pasta you use and the brand), drain it in a colander placed in the sink and then return it to the pot. Discard the bay leaf from the sauce for the ribs, then spoon some of the sauce over the pasta and toss thoroughly.

Serve the pasta in shallow bowls dressed with additional sauce, some of the meat, and the cheese.

OSSO BUCO IN SALSA BRUNA

¼ ounce (¼ cup) dried porcini mushrooms

½ cup boiling water

2 tablespoons extra-virgin olive oil

2 tablespoons unsalted butter

6 meaty, bone-in veal shanks, each about 8 ounces and 1½ inches thick

All-purpose flour for dredging

Kosher or sea salt

Freshly ground black pepper

1 cup dry white wine

1 large or 2 medium yellow onions, coarsely chopped (about 2 cups)

2 carrots, peeled and coarsely chopped

2 ribs celery, trimmed and coarsely chopped

¼ cup finely chopped fresh flat-leaf parsley

5 whole cloves

4 small sprigs fresh thyme

2 fresh bay leaves

½ teaspoon black peppercorns

2½ cups *Sostanzioso Brodo di Manzo* (page 25) or best-quality canned low-sodium beef broth, or as needed

1½ ounces thinly sliced *prosciutto di Parma*, cut crosswise into narrow ribbons

¼ cup dry Marsala

Risotto allo Zafferano (see variation, page 152) for serving

In the 1970s, for several years in a row, my mother made hundreds of batches of this succulent veal stew—her unique version of osso buco—as part of a fund-raiser for my school. She manned the food booth at the school's annual Christmas bazaar, and every year orders for this and her other creations would pile up weeks before the event. My mother always serves this with Risotto allo Zafferano (see variation, page 152). If you are an adventurous eater, you'll want to use a small spoon or the tip of a knife to get the rich marrow inside the shank bone. It's my favorite part.

MAKES 4 TO 6 MAIN-COURSE SERVINGS

Put the porcini in a small heatproof bowl and pour the boiling water over them. Let soak for 20 to 30 minutes, or until softened. Drain the porcini in a fine-mesh sieve lined with damp paper towels or cheesecloth, reserving the liquid. Chop the mushrooms coarsely and set the mushrooms and liquid aside separately.

While the porcini are soaking, heat 1 tablespoon each of the olive oil and butter in a large Dutch oven or other heavy-bottomed pot with a lid over medium-high heat. Dredge the veal shanks in the flour, shaking off any excess. When the oil is hot, place 3 or 4 shanks in the pot and sprinkle them with a little salt and pepper. Sear for about 4 minutes, or until golden brown on the first side. Turn with tongs and brown for about 4 minutes on the other side, sprinkling them with a little more salt and pepper. Remove them to a shallow bowl or plate. Repeat with the remaining shanks, salting and peppering each batch. When the last batch is removed, pour in ½ cup of the wine and deglaze the pot, stirring to scrape up any browned bits from the bottom. Let the wine bubble for a minute or two and then pour it over the shanks and set aside.

Heat the oven to 325 degrees F.

Add the remaining 1 tablespoon each of the oil and butter to the pot over medium heat. Add the onions, carrots, celery, parsley, chopped porcini, cloves, thyme, bay leaves, and peppercorns. Sauté the vegetables, stirring frequently, for 8 to 10 minutes, or until they have softened. Pour in a splash of the remaining ½ cup wine and let it evaporate as you stir the vegetables. Pour in another splash and stir until it is evaporated, and then pour in the rest. Season with a little salt and then stir in 1 cup of the broth and the porcini liquid. Cover partially and simmer the vegetables over medium heat for about 30 minutes, or until they are completely soft and browned. Remove from the heat. Using tongs or a fork, remove and discard the bay leaves, thyme sprigs, and the 5 cloves. You may have to fish around a bit for the cloves, but it won't take more than a minute. Leave in the peppercorns. Let cool for about 5 minutes.

In a blender or food processor, purée the vegetable mixture until smooth. Pour the puréed vegetables into the same pot in which you cooked them and stir in the remaining 1½ cups broth. Lay the browned shanks in the sauce and tip in the juices from the platter. The sauce should just cover the shanks; if not, add a splash more broth. Scatter the prosciutto over all. Cover and place the pot in the oven. Cook for 1 hour.

Uncover, raise the oven heat to 350 degrees F, and cook for 1 more hour. Sprinkle the Marsala over the veal, re-cover, and let cook for another 5 to 10 minutes. The stew is done when the sauce is thick and a fork glides easily into the meat.

Serve the stew in individual shallow bowls, with the risotto as an accompaniment.

SPEZZATINO AL GINEPRO

3½ pounds boneless chuck roast, cut into 1½-inch cubes

FOR THE MARINADE

1 small yellow onion, thinly sliced

1 carrot, peeled and coarsely chopped

1 large rib celery, including leafy top, trimmed and coarsely chopped

4 small fresh sprigs rosemary, or 1 large fresh rosemary sprig, 6 inches long, broken into 4 pieces

6 fresh sage leaves

2 fresh bay leaves

4 sprigs fresh flat-leaf parsley

1 tablespoon juniper berries, lightly bruised to release their aroma

1 teaspoon black peppercorns

1 bottle (750 milliliter) Chianti

FOR THE STEW

2 to 4 tablespoons extra-virgin olive oil

1 large or 2 medium yellow onions, finely chopped (about 2 cups)

1 carrot, peeled and finely chopped

1 large clove garlic, passed through a garlic press

1 teaspoon kosher or sea salt

1 sprig fresh rosemary

½ teaspoon juniper berries

Risotto allo Zafferano (see variation, page 152), *Polenta di Frumentino* (see variation, page 154), or Italian country bread for serving

This hearty beef stew is perfumed with woodsy herbs and aromatic juniper berries. It is an adaptation of a dish I had one cold, misty afternoon in Assisi, at a restaurant near the Basilica of Saint Francis. That version featured cinghiale, or wild boar, rather than beef. Cinghiale is truly a treat; it's pork with oomph. The meat is darker, leaner, and tastier than standard pork. While wild boar is increasingly turning up on American restaurant menus, it is still unavailable at most supermarket meat counters. I use beef here, but regular pork would work nicely, too.

MAKES 6 MAIN-COURSE SERVINGS

TO MARINATE THE MEAT:

Put the meat in a large Dutch oven or other nonreactive vessel. Scatter the onion, carrot, celery, herbs, crushed juniper berries, and peppercorns over the meat and pour in the wine. Stir gently to combine the ingredients. Cover tightly and refrigerate for 24 to 48 hours.

Remove the meat pieces from the marinade and pat dry with paper towels. Pour the liquid through a fine-mesh sieve placed over a bowl and discard the solids. Reserve the meat and liquid separately.

TO MAKE THE STEW:

In a large Dutch oven, heat 2 tablespoons olive oil over medium-high heat. Working in batches, add the meat and sear, turning the pieces with tongs as needed, for about 5 minutes, or until evenly browned on all sides. As the batches are browned, use a slotted spoon to remove them to a bowl.

If little or no oil remains in the pot after browning the meat, add another 2 tablespoons olive oil over medium heat. Stir in the onion and carrot and sauté for 5 minutes, or until the vegetables are shiny and just beginning to soften. In a small bowl, mix together the mashed garlic and salt to form a paste and add the paste to the vegetables. Stir well and cook for a minute or two, or until the garlic releases its fragrance. Return the meat to the pot and add the rosemary sprig and juniper berries. Pour in the reserved marinade liquid. It should just cover the meat. If it doesn't, add water as needed to barely cover. Bring the stew to a boil over medium-high heat and skim off any foam that forms on the surface with a skimmer.

Reduce the heat to low, cover partially, and simmer gently for 2½ to 3 hours, or until the meat is very tender and the liquid has turned into a dark, thick sauce.

Serve the stew in a large, deep serving platter or in individual shallow bowls, spooned over risotto or polenta, or with fresh country bread on the side.

Oven-Braised Endive

INDIVIA BRASATA AL FORNO

1 tablespoon unsalted butter, plus more for preparing baking dish

6 heads Belgian endive

1 tablespoon extra-virgin olive oil

1 carrot, peeled and finely chopped

1 rib celery, trimmed and finely chopped

2 ounces pancetta, minced

1 clove garlic, passed through a garlic press

½ teaspoon kosher or sea salt

Freshly ground black pepper

¼ cup dry white wine

¾ cup canned whole tomatoes, diced

⅔ cup freshly grated *Parmigiano-Reggiano* cheese

Braising endive transforms it from a crisp, bitter salad green into a silky-textured winter vegetable with a mellow, slightly nutty flavor. It makes a satisfying side dish to sautéed or panfried fish, roast chicken, or chicken cutlets. As good as it is straight out of the oven, braised endive may be even better as leftovers. My daughter, Adriana, and I have been known to eat it for lunch, cold from the fridge or at room temperature, spooned over grilled bread.

MAKES 6 SIDE-DISH SERVINGS

Heat the oven to 350 degrees F. Butter a rectangular baking dish large enough to hold the endives in one layer.

Trim the stem end off each endive and discard any discolored or soft outer leaves. Cut each endive in half lengthwise.

In a large skillet, heat the olive oil and butter over medium heat. When the butter has melted and begins to sizzle, add the endive halves, cut side down. Brown for 4 minutes; turn and brown the other side for 4 minutes. Transfer the endive halves, cut side up (along with any stray leaves that may have come detached), to the prepared baking dish and set aside.

Return the skillet to medium heat and add the carrot, celery, and pancetta. Sauté for about 5 minutes, or until the pancetta has rendered its fat and the vegetables have begun to soften. In a small bowl, mix together the garlic and salt to form a paste and add the paste to the vegetables. Stir to combine well. Season the vegetables with pepper to taste and continue to sauté for a few more minutes, or until the garlic has released its fragrance. Increase the heat to medium-high and pour in the wine. Cook for 2 minutes, or until some of the wine has evaporated. Add the tomatoes and cook for 5 minutes to allow the flavors to mingle. Taste and adjust the seasoning with salt and pepper. Pour the sauce over the endives in the baking dish.

Cover the baking dish with aluminum foil, place in the oven, and braise for 1 hour. Uncover, sprinkle evenly with the cheese, return the baking dish to the oven, and cook for 20 minutes, or until the cheese has melted and turned golden brown.

Remove from the oven and let cool for 5 to 10 minutes. Serve the endives directly from the baking dish.

CHAPTER 4

PRIMAVERA
Recipes for Spring

98 Crespelle in Brodo
Crêpes in Broth

99 Zuppa alla Pavese
Poached Egg Soup from Pavia

100 Minestra della Nonna
Nonna's Chicken Soup

101 Minestra del Pastore
Shepherd's Soup

103 Vellutata di Asparagi con Orzo Perlato
Cream of Asparagus Soup with Pearled Barley

105 Crema di Piselli alla Maggiorana
Sweet Pea Soup with Marjoram

106 Minestra di Lattuga e Riso
Lettuce and Rice Soup

107 Maccù
Spring Cleaning Soup

108 Zuppa di Vongole al Prosecco
Clam Stew with Prosecco

110 Gamberetti Piccanti in Umido
Spicy Shrimp Stew

111 Stufato di Pollo con Scarola e Porri
Smothered Chicken with Escarole and Leeks

113 Spezzatino di Agnello e Patate
Lamb and Potato Stew

115 Stracotto di Manzo alla Gabriella
Gabriella's Pot Roast

117 Stufato di Carciofi con Lattuga e Piselli
Artichoke Stew with Lettuce and Peas

119 Bietola con le Patate
Swiss Chard and Potatoes

S pring likes to play games. One week it is 75 degrees and the cherry trees are beckoning us outdoors with lacy blossoms. The next week we are forced back inside by a cold, incessant drizzle. In such a temperamental season, flexibility is your friend in the kitchen.

Happily, there are soups and stews to match all of spring's moods. Soups can be as hearty as *Maccu*, a traditional Sicilian soup of mixed dried legumes that is more a farewell to winter than a salute to spring; or as light as *Crespelle in Brodo*, an old-fashioned soup from Abruzzo that floats paper-thin rolled egg crêpes in homemade chicken broth. Velvety purées of asparagus or peas, at once rich and light, offer a chance to savor the delicate flavors of the season's star vegetables.

There are plenty of evenings in spring when a good pot roast is the main event at my table. My mother's classic recipe, with finely chopped carrots, celery, and onion, has plenty of substance, but with no potatoes it is also a shade lighter than a typical winter pot roast. Just as welcome is an earthy stew of artichokes laced with fresh peas and wilted lettuce, accompanied by a wedge of cheese and good bread.

CRESPELLE IN BRODO

FOR THE CRÊPE BATTER

4 large eggs

1 cup goat's milk or whole cow's milk

2 tablespoons minced fresh flat-leaf parsley

½ teaspoon kosher or sea salt

Pinch of freshly ground black pepper

Pinch of freshly grated nutmeg

¾ cup unbleached all-purpose flour, sifted

8 to 9 cups (2 to 2¼ quarts) *Brodo di Pollo* (page 24)

About 2 tablespoons unsalted butter

2 cups freshly grated *pecorino romano* cheese, plus more for serving (optional)

COOK'S NOTE:

If you're making the crêpes ahead of time, stack them as you make them; cover them tightly with plastic and store in the refrigerator for up to 3 days (or in the freezer for up to a month). Bring them to room temperature before proceeding with the recipe.

I sometimes like to make a less fancy variation of this soup: Do not sprinkle the crêpes with cheese. Instead, roll up the plain crêpes and cut them crosswise into thin ribbons (⅛ to ¼ inch wide). Unraveled, they resemble fine egg noodles. Cook the strips in boiling broth for just a couple of minutes, or until they are heated through. Ladle the soup into bowls and sprinkle with pecorino.

This is a classic recipe from my mother's home region of Abruzzo. I like to serve it on Easter Sunday, with roast lamb as the main course, but it makes a lovely first course for nearly any dinner party. Thin egg crêpes are sprinkled with sharp pecorino cheese, rolled into cigars, arranged in soup plates, and then hot broth is ladled over them. I use goat's milk for the crêpe batter because I like the way it subtly echoes the sheep's milk flavor of the pecorino, but regular cow's milk is fine, too. Both the crêpes and the broth can be made ahead of time and stored in the refrigerator or freezer, making the soup perfect stress-free party fare. If you have never made crêpes before, you will be pleasantly surprised at how easy it is.

MAKES 6 FIRST-COURSE SERVINGS

TO MAKE THE CRÊPE BATTER:

In a bowl, whisk together the eggs, milk, parsley, salt, pepper, and nutmeg. Gradually whisk in the flour, taking care to avoid lumps. Cover the batter with plastic wrap and let stand at room temperature for 30 minutes.

In a saucepan, bring the broth to a simmer over medium heat.

While the broth is heating, cook the crêpes: In a 9-inch nonstick skillet (I use a well-seasoned cast-iron skillet), melt a little of the butter—just enough to film the bottom—over medium heat. When the butter is hot, pour in a small ladleful of crêpe batter—less than ½ cup—and quickly swirl the pan so that the batter coats the bottom, forming a thin pancake. Cook for 30 to 45 seconds, or until just set and barely beginning to brown on the bottom. Then, using an offset spatula, flip the crêpe and cook on the second side for 20 to 30 seconds, or until set. Transfer the crêpe to a plate. Continue making crêpes until you have used all the batter, making sure to add butter to the pan as needed so that the bottom is always coated with a thin film. Stack the crêpes on the plate as you remove them from the pan. You should end up with 12 crêpes.

Sprinkle a little of the pecorino cheese—about 3 tablespoons—on each crêpe and roll up the crêpe into a cigar shape. As the crêpes are rolled, place them, seam side down, in shallow bowls, putting 2 crêpes in each bowl.

Ladle the hot broth over the crêpes and sprinkle with additional pecorino, if you like.

ZUPPA ALLA PAVESE

6 cups *Brodo di Carne* (page 26)

3 tablespoons unsalted butter

4 slices day-old Italian bread, each ¾ inch thick

4 very fresh large eggs

8 tablespoons freshly grated *Parmigiano-Reggiano* cheese

COOK'S NOTE:
If you would like the eggs a little more cooked, use flameproof bowls (place them on a rimmed baking sheet), and after filling them with the bread, eggs, cheese, and broth, run them under a heated broiler for 30 to 60 seconds, or just until the egg whites are opaque but the yolks are still soft and tender.

For this delicate yet substantial soup from Italy's northern Lombardy region, you will need the freshest eggs you can find. Toasted bread slices are placed on the bottom of shallow soup plates and then eggs are cracked open—with the utmost care so as not to break the yolks—onto the slices. When boiling broth is poured carefully around the bread and eggs, the eggs are gently "poached" (see Cook's Note).

MAKES 4 FIRST-COURSE SERVINGS

In a saucepan, bring the broth to a boil over medium-high heat.

While the broth is heating, in a large skillet, melt the butter over medium heat. When the butter has melted and begins to sizzle and foam, add the bread slices and fry for about 2 minutes, or until the bottom side is golden brown around the edges and pale gold in the center. Turn the slices over and fry the second side for another minute or so or until the bottom side is golden brown around the edges and pale gold in the center.

Place the bread slices in 4 shallow soup bowls. Carefully crack an egg over each bread slice, taking care to keep the yolk intact. (Your goal is for the egg yolk to be positioned right on the bread, but slippery eggs sometimes have a mind of their own and this trick is difficult to get right every time. Don't worry about it—if the yolk is intact you've done well.)

Sprinkle 1 tablespoon of the cheese over each egg. Carefully ladle the boiling broth into the bowls, pouring it around the egg yolks rather than directly over them. Sprinkle each bowl with an additional 1 tablespoon cheese.

Nonna's Chicken Soup

MINESTRA DELLA NONNA

My father's mother, Maria De Rita Marchetti, was born in Isernia, south of Rome, but lived most of her life in Cranston, Rhode Island. My sister and I called her Nonna Rhode Island to distinguish her from our maternal grandmother, Maria Petrosemolo Tomassoni, who lived in Italy, and whom we called Nonna Italy. Whenever we drove up from New Jersey to visit our New England relatives, Nonna Rhode Island had a pot ready of this nutritious, comforting chicken soup with pieces of broken noodles, lots of tiny meatballs, and shreds of escarole or spinach. My daughter, Adriana, loves rolling the tiny meatballs, and her little hands are the perfect size for the task.

MAKES 10 FIRST-COURSE SERVINGS

FOR THE MEATBALLS

- 1½ cups fresh bread crumbs (see Cook's Note)
- ½ cup whole milk, heated to warm
- 5 ounces ground beef
- 5 ounces ground pork
- 5 ounces ground veal
- 1 large egg, lightly beaten
- ½ cup freshly grated *Parmigiano-Reggiano* cheese
- 1 clove garlic, passed through a garlic press
- 1 tablespoon minced fresh flat-leaf parsley
- ½ teaspoon kosher or sea salt

FOR THE SOUP

- 10 cups *Brodo di Pollo* (page 24)
- 1 small head escarole, washed, trimmed, and coarsely shredded, or 8 ounces spinach leaves, washed and trimmed
- 3 cups thin dried pasta noodles such as capellini, broken into 1-inch pieces

Freshly grated *Parmigiano-Reggiano* cheese for serving

COOK'S NOTE:

To make the bread crumbs, cut away the crusts from 3 or 4 thick slices of fresh or day-old Italian country bread. Tear the slices into 2-inch chunks, place in a food processor, and pulse until coarse crumbs form. Measure out 1½ cups to use for the meatballs; reserve any left over for another use.

TO MAKE THE MEATBALLS:

In a bowl, combine the bread crumbs and milk and let sit for about 15 minutes, or until the bread has absorbed all the liquid.

Line a large baking sheet or platter with waxed paper. In a large bowl, combine the ground meats, milk-soaked bread, egg, cheese, garlic, parsley, and salt. Mix with your hands or a wooden spoon until the ingredients are thoroughly combined. Dampen your hands with cold water, pinch off a small piece (about 1 teaspoon) of the meatball mixture, and roll it into a ball. Place on the prepared baking sheet. Continue to form the meatballs until you have used all the mixture. Keep your hands moistened with cold water to prevent the mixture from sticking to them. You should end up with about 200 meatballs.

TO MAKE THE SOUP:

Bring the broth to a boil in a large saucepot placed over medium heat. Carefully add the meatballs and greens and simmer for about 10 minutes, or until the meatballs are just cooked and the greens have wilted. Stir in the pasta and let the soup boil until the pasta is al dente; the cooking time will vary depending on which pasta you use and the brand.

Ladle the hot soup into shallow bowls and sprinkle each serving with the cheese.

Shepherd's Soup

MINESTRA DEL PASTORE

3 cups water

3 cups goat's milk or whole cow's milk

2 teaspoons kosher or sea salt, or to taste

2 cups cut-up green beans (1-inch pieces)

2½ cups peeled, diced yellow-fleshed potatoes such as Yukon gold (1-inch dice)

1¼ cups broken spaghetti (1-inch pieces)

½ cup fresh or frozen shelled English peas

1 cup freshly grated *pecorino romano* cheese

This recipe was given to me by my friend Melchiorre Chessa, who was born on Sardinia but moved to Umbria, in central Italy, when he was a youngster. This soup was a favorite of his as a child, and indeed its gentle flavor and nourishing qualities are perfect for children. Tender vegetables and broken spaghetti are simmered in a soothing milk-based broth. In Italy, Melchiorre makes this soup with fresh sheep's milk, an ingredient that is hard to come by here unless you own a herd of sheep or know someone who does. An excellent substitute is goat's milk, available at many supermarkets and health-food stores, though cow's milk will do in a pinch.

MAKES 4 FIRST-COURSE SERVINGS

In a medium Dutch oven or saucepot, combine the water and milk and bring almost to a boil over medium-high heat (watch that the liquid does not boil over). Add the salt and green beans, reduce the heat to medium, and boil for 3 minutes. Add the potatoes and boil for another 3 minutes, or until they are just tender. Stir in the pasta and boil gently for about 15 minutes, or until the pasta is al dente. Stir in the peas and cook for 2 to 3 minutes if using frozen or slightly longer if using fresh, or until just tender.

While the peas are cooking, put the cheese in a small bowl and add a few spoonfuls of the milky broth. Stir the cheese and hot broth together to make a thin paste and stir the paste into the soup until fully incorporated.

To serve, ladle the soup into shallow bowls.

VELLUTATA DI ASPARAGI CON ORZO PERLATO

6 cups water

Kosher or sea salt

1 cup pearled barley, rinsed

2 pounds asparagus

2 tablespoons extra-virgin olive oil

1 tablespoon unsalted butter

2 spring onions, bulbs and tender white part of stalks sliced crosswise (about 1 cup) (see Cook's Note)

1 fennel bulb, trimmed, quartered lengthwise, and quarters thinly sliced crosswise

2 tablespoons all-purpose flour

6 cups *Brodo di Magro* (page 27), *Brodo di Pollo* (page 24), or best-quality canned low-sodium chicken broth, heated to a simmer

6 sprigs fresh flat-leaf parsley

Freshly ground black pepper

1 cup freshly grated *pecorino romano* cheese

COOK'S NOTE:

The spring onions I'm referring to are not scallions, but rather young bulb onions still attached to their stalks. Both red and white ones are available in many well-stocked supermarkets in the spring. If you can't find them, substitute 2 leeks, using the bulb and tender, light green part of the stalks.

Tender, grassy green asparagus, aromatic spring onions, and sweet fennel mingle harmoniously in this soup honoring the first flavors of the season. Adding pearled barley to the mix gives it a little more substance. Accompany the soup with country bread for a nice one-dish supper.

MAKES 6 FIRST-COURSE SERVINGS

Put the barley on to cook before you start the soup: In a large saucepan, combine the water and 1 teaspoon salt and bring to a boil over high heat. Slowly pour in the barley. Reduce the heat to medium and simmer for 45 minutes, or until the barley is tender but still a bit chewy. It should not be mushy at all. Reduce the heat if necessary so that the barley cooks at a gentle, steady simmer. Drain the barley in a colander placed in the sink and let it sit for 10 minutes. Fluff with a fork and set aside.

While the barley is cooking, trim off the tough ends from the asparagus and discard them (or add them to the pot in which you are heating the stock to enhance its flavor; remove them before adding the stock to the soup). Cut the asparagus stalks into 1-inch pieces. Set aside the tips. You should have about 4½ cups asparagus pieces, not including the tips.

In a large Dutch oven or other heavy-bottomed pot, heat the oil and butter over medium heat. Add the spring onions and fennel, reduce the heat to medium-low, and sauté, stirring from time to time, for about 10 minutes, or until the vegetables are softened. Sprinkle the flour over the vegetables and stir vigorously to combine. Pour in 1 cup of the stock and stir for a minute or so to incorporate thoroughly. Slowly pour in the remaining 5 cups of stock and add the asparagus pieces—except for the reserved tips—and the parsley sprigs. Increase the heat to medium and simmer for 15 to 20 minutes, until all the vegetables are tender. Remove from the heat and let the soup cool for 10 minutes.

In a blender, working in batches, purée the soup. Strain the soup through a fine-mesh sieve to remove any tough fibers and return it to the pot. Stir in the cooked barley and reheat the soup over low heat. Season to taste with salt and pepper.

CONTINUED

Meanwhile, put the reserved asparagus tips in a steaming basket placed in a pot of boiling water, cover, and steam for 4 to 5 minutes, or just until tender. Alternatively, put the tips in a plastic storage bag along with 1 tablespoon water. Set the open bag in a microwave oven and cook on high for 3 minutes, or until the tips are bright green and just tender.

To serve the soup, stir in ¾ cup of the cheese. Ladle the soup into a large serving bowl or tureen and top with the reserved asparagus tips and the remaining ¼ cup cheese. You can also serve the soup in individual bowls, garnishing each serving with a few asparagus tips and a sprinkle of cheese.

Sweet Pea Soup with Marjoram

CREMA DI PISELLI ALLA MAGGIORANA

2 tablespoons extra-virgin olive oil

1 cup thinly sliced leeks, white and light green parts only

1 small sprig fresh marjoram

1 small sprig fresh thyme

4 cups *Brodo di Pollo* (page 24) or best-quality canned low-sodium chicken broth

4 cups shelled English peas (about 4 pounds in the pod)

¼ cup heavy cream

½ teaspoon kosher or sea salt, or to taste

Freshly ground black pepper

Mascarpone cheese or crème fraîche for serving (optional)

This light soup is nothing like its heavy winter cousin, split-pea soup. Fresh marjoram imparts a delicate perfume and a touch of cream provides a velvety texture. Little hands are perfect for shelling fresh peas, so I usually put my kids to work when I make this. My son, Nick, turns the event into a race with his younger sister who, intentionally or not, ignores the competition taking place and proceeds at her own idle pace.

MAKES 4 FIRST-COURSE SERVINGS

In a large Dutch oven or other heavy-bottomed pot, heat the olive oil over medium heat. Add the leeks and sauté, stirring frequently, for about 3 minutes, or until they have softened and are translucent but not browned. Add the marjoram and thyme and sauté for 1 minute while stirring. Pour in the broth, raise the heat to medium-high, and bring to a simmer. Carefully tip in the peas and cook for 6 to 8 minutes, or until they are just tender. Remove from the heat, remove and discard the sprigs of marjoram and thyme, and let the soup cool for 10 minutes.

In a food processor or blender, working in batches if necessary, purée the soup until smooth. If you want a perfectly smooth soup, strain it through a medium-mesh sieve lined with cheesecloth and discard the solids.

Return the soup to the pot and place over medium heat. Stir in the cream, add the salt, and season to taste with pepper. Heat until just warmed through.

Ladle the soup into shallow bowls and garnish, if you like, with a dollop of mascarpone cheese.

Lettuce and Rice Soup

MINESTRA DI LATTUGA E RISO

2 tablespoons unsalted butter

2 tablespoons extra-virgin olive oil

1 carrot, peeled and finely chopped

1 rib celery, trimmed and finely chopped

1 small yellow onion, finely chopped

1 tablespoon minced fresh flat-leaf parsley

1 teaspoon kosher or sea salt, or to taste

1 small head butter lettuce, washed, trimmed, and shredded

1 small head romaine lettuce, washed, trimmed, and shredded

1 small head escarole, washed, trimmed, and shredded

4 cups baby spinach leaves, washed

6 cups *Brodo di Pollo* (page 24) or *Brodo di Magro* (page 27), or best-quality canned low-sodium chicken broth, heated to a simmer

1 cup Arborio or long-grain white rice

Freshly ground black pepper

½ cup thinly shaved *Parmigiano-Reggiano* cheese

Every spoonful of this soup, with its tender morsels of carrot and shredded greens, is a welcome taste of spring. Rice and thinly shaved Parmigiano-Reggiano cheese add just enough heft. The greens lose their bright green hue when you cook them. The earthy appearance doesn't bother me, as it reminds me of the many wonderful versions of this classic soup I enjoyed as a child. But if you want to perk up the color, gently stir in another handful or two of spinach during the last few minutes of cooking.

MAKES 6 FIRST-COURSE SERVINGS

In a Dutch oven or other heavy-bottomed pot with a lid, heat the butter and oil over medium heat. When the butter has melted and begins to sizzle, add the carrot, celery, onion, and parsley and sauté for about 10 minutes, or until the vegetables have begun to soften and the onion is translucent. Season with the salt and then stir in the butter and romaine lettuces, escarole, and spinach, tossing the greens so that they are all well coated with the other ingredients. Cook, stirring from time to time, for 5 minutes or so, or until the greens have wilted.

Pour in the broth, stir in the rice, and bring the soup to a boil over medium-high heat. Reduce the heat to low, cover, and simmer gently for 18 minutes, or until the rice is cooked. Taste and adjust the seasoning with salt, remembering that cheese will add saltiness, too.

Ladle the soup into a tureen. Garnish with a few grinds of black pepper and the cheese.

MACCU

2½ cups mixed dried beans including
1 cup dried fava beans and 1½ cups
other beans, such as chickpeas
and kidney beans, soaked overnight in
water to cover

½ cup green or yellow split peas, rinsed
and drained

¼ cup brown lentils, rinsed and drained

¼ cup red lentils, rinsed and drained

2½ quarts (10 cups) water

2 ribs celery, trimmed and finely
chopped

1 small fennel bulb, trimmed and finely
chopped

1 yellow onion, halved and finely
chopped

1 bunch Swiss chard, washed, trimmed,
leaves cut crosswise into strips, and
stems chopped

¼ cup extra-virgin olive oil

Kosher or sea salt

Generous pinch of red pepper flakes

Best-quality extra-virgin olive oil for
serving

Maccu, a Sicilian soup made with long-cooked dried fava beans and other legumes, is traditionally served on March 19 to celebrate the feast of Saint Joseph. It has long been thought of as a good way for Sicilian housewives to rid their pantries of any dried legumes left over from winter, which is why I named this variation Spring Cleaning Soup. The fava beans are a must in this dish; they fall apart during the more than 3 hours of simmering, giving the soup lots of body, a good thing on a raw day in late March.

MAKES 8 FIRST-COURSE SERVINGS OR 4 TO 6 MAIN-COURSE SERVINGS

Drain the beans and put them in a large Dutch oven or soup pot with a lid. Add the split peas, brown and red lentils, and the water. Bring to a boil over medium-high heat, skimming any foam that forms on the surface with a skimmer. Reduce the heat to medium-low, cover partially, and simmer for 1½ hours, or until the beans are somewhat tender.

Add the celery, fennel, onion, and chard and stir well to combine everything thoroughly. Pour in the ¼ cup olive oil and season with a little salt and the red pepper flakes. Continue to simmer, partially covered, for another 1½ to 2 hours, or until all the legumes and the vegetables are very tender and the soup is thick. Add more water if the soup seems too dense, but remember it should be nearly thick enough to hold a wooden spoon upright. Taste for salt and add more if necessary.

Ladle the soup into shallow bowls and drizzle each serving with your best olive oil.

Clam Stew with Prosecco

ZUPPA DI VONGOLE AL PROSECCO

2 cloves garlic, sliced paper-thin

2 small dried red chili peppers, crumbled, or a generous pinch of red pepper flakes

⅓ cup extra-virgin olive oil

1 cup Prosecco or dry white wine

48 littleneck or other small clams, thoroughly cleaned (page 16)

Kosher or sea salt

2 tablespoons finely chopped fresh flat-leaf parsley, or more to taste

8 slices *Crostini* (page 148) or 4 slices *Bruschetta* (page 151)

Best-quality extra-virgin olive oil for serving

Prosecco is a dry, mildly sparkling white wine from the Veneto region. I use it here because, in all honesty, it was the only white wine I had on hand one day when I was making this simple, classic southern Italian stew. It turned out to be a perfect match for the clams, enhancing their briny sea flavor without over-whelming it. I have, at various times, tried to soup up this recipe by adding shallots, chopped fresh tomatoes, mixed fresh herbs, or even diced pancetta. But I always come back to this most basic and, in my opinion, most delicious version. Here, less is truly more; the fewer ingredients you use, the more the flavor of the clams will shine through.

MAKES 4 MAIN-COURSE SERVINGS

In a large skillet or sauté pan, warm the garlic and chili peppers in the ⅓ cup olive oil over medium heat until the garlic just starts to sizzle. Do not let it brown or it will become bitter.

Increase the heat to medium-high and add the Prosecco (it will foam briefly) and the clams and toss. Cover the pan and steam the clams for 5 to 10 minutes, or until they open. Taste the broth and add salt if necessary—this will depend on the saltiness of the clam liquor. Turn off the heat and stir in the parsley. Discard any clams that failed to open.

Arrange the bread at the bottom of 4 shallow bowls, dividing it evenly. Divide the clams and broth evenly among the bowls, ladling them over the bread. Drizzle with your best olive oil.

Spicy Shrimp Stew

GAMBERETTI PICCANTI
IN UMIDO

2 cloves garlic, passed through a garlic press

1 small sprig fresh rosemary, finely chopped

1 teaspoon kosher or sea salt

1 tablespoon extra-virgin olive oil

1 tablespoon fatback or pancetta, finely minced or ground

1 bunch scallions (about 6), ends trimmed and white and green parts thinly sliced crosswise

½ cup dry white wine

Generous pinch of red pepper flakes

1 pound medium shrimp, peeled and deveined (page 16)

Freshly ground black pepper

4 to 6 slices *Bruschetta* (page 151)

Here is proof that not all stews take hours to cook. This recipe is fast, easy to prepare, and delicious. It comes from my Sardinian friend Melchiorre Chessa, who prepared it one night as an appetizer, with toasted bread on the side. I loved it so much that I turned it into a main course. Make it whichever way you prefer. When it comes to shrimp, I am usually a bigger-is-better person, but for this recipe I prefer the bite-sized medium shrimp, and even small ones if you're making it as an appetizer. P.S.: Don't leave out the fatback. It's only a small amount but it makes all the difference. Serve the stew with steamed asparagus or a tossed green salad on the side.
MAKES 2 TO 3 MAIN-COURSE SERVINGS

In a small bowl, mix together the garlic, rosemary, and salt to form a paste. Set aside.

In a skillet, heat the oil and fatback over medium to medium-high heat. When the fatback begins to turn translucent and melt, add the scallions and sauté for a minute or so, or until the scallions are well coated. Stir in the garlic-rosemary paste and cook for another minute or two, or until the garlic and rosemary begin to release their fragrance. Pour in ¼ cup of the wine, cover the skillet, and cook for 2 minutes. Sprinkle in the red pepper flakes, cover, and cook for a little longer, or until the scallions are softened and have somewhat darkened. Add the shrimp and cook, uncovered, for a minute or two, or until they are opaque. Add the remaining ¼ cup wine and a couple of grinds of black pepper. Cook for another minute or two, or until the shrimp are pink and just cooked through.

Taste and adjust the seasoning with salt. Ladle the stew into shallow bowls and serve the *bruschetta* alongside.

Smothered Chicken with Escarole and Leeks

STUFATO DI POLLO CON SCAROLA E PORRI

4 tablespoons unsalted butter

3 leeks, white and light green parts, washed, trimmed, and cut into thin rounds

4 to 5 small sprigs fresh thyme

1 chicken, 4 pounds, cut into 10 serving pieces

Kosher or sea salt

Freshly ground black pepper

2 heads escarole, washed, trimmed, and coarsely chopped or shredded

Juice of ½ lemon

Every time I make this recipe I am amazed that such a plain list of ingredients can yield such a delectable, savory result. Escarole is a popular ingredient in Italian cooking, particularly in soups and stews. My mother also serves it boiled, dressed with good olive oil, lemon juice, and salt. Here, the escarole is gradually transformed from a rather tough salad green into a thick, pulpy sauce rich with the flavors of the chicken and leeks. I like to serve this stew spooned over long-grain rice that has been cooked in chicken broth with a little salt and butter.

MAKES 4 MAIN-COURSE SERVINGS

In a large sauté pan with a lid, melt the butter over medium heat. When the butter has melted and begins to sizzle, add the leeks and thyme and sauté, stirring from time to time, for about 5 minutes, or until the leeks have softened. Add the chicken pieces, skin side down, arranging them among the leeks. Season with salt and pepper and let the chicken brown for 10 minutes. Turn the chicken pieces skin side up and season with additional salt and pepper. Scatter the escarole over the chicken, cover the pan, and reduce the heat to medium-low. Simmer, stirring occasionally, for 50 to 60 minutes, or until the chicken is cooked through and the escarole has been reduced to a thick sauce.

Uncover, raise the heat to medium, and sprinkle the lemon juice over the chicken. Stir and cook for about 4 minutes longer, or until the lemon juice has been well incorporated into the sauce, and then serve.

Lamb and Potato Stew

SPEZZATINO DI AGNELLO E PATATE

2 tablespoons extra-virgin olive oil, plus more if needed

2 pounds boneless lamb stew meat (leg or shoulder), cut into 1-inch cubes

1 carrot, peeled and finely chopped

1 rib celery, trimmed and finely chopped

2 cloves garlic, passed through a garlic press

½ teaspoon kosher or sea salt

1 tablespoon minced fresh oregano

½ cup dry white wine

4 yellow-fleshed potatoes such as Yukon gold, about 2 pounds total weight, peeled and cut into 1-inch cubes

2 cups canned whole tomatoes, passed through a food mill fitted with the plate with medium-sized holes

Generous pinch of red pepper flakes

2 tablespoons minced fresh flat-leaf parsley

Make this stew in early spring, on a day when the weather is chilly and damp. The spicy sauce will warm you right up. My favorite part of this dish might be the potatoes because they soak up all the rich flavors of the meat and tomatoes. Serve Italian country bread alongside.

MAKES 4 MAIN-COURSE SERVINGS

In a large Dutch oven or other heavy-bottomed pot with a lid, heat the 2 tablespoons olive oil over medium-high heat. When the oil is hot, arrange the lamb cubes on the bottom of the pot and sear, turning as needed, for 8 to 10 minutes, or until browned on all sides. Remove the browned meat to a bowl.

If there is little or no fat left in the pot, add another 2 tablespoons oil. Add the carrot and celery and sauté, stirring, for about 5 minutes, or until somewhat softened. In a small bowl, mix together the garlic, salt, and oregano to form a paste. Add the paste to the vegetables and sauté for a minute or two longer, or just until the garlic is fragrant. Return the meat to the pot, along with any juices that have accumulated in the bowl. Pour in the wine and cook for a couple of minutes, or until some of the wine has evaporated. Add the potatoes and stir to combine with the other ingredients. Pour in the tomatoes and season with the red pepper flakes. Bring the stew to a boil, reduce the heat to medium-low, cover, and simmer for 1½ hours, or until the meat is very tender (reduce the heat to low if necessary to maintain a gentle simmer).

Taste and adjust the seasoning with salt and remove from the heat. Stir in the parsley, then ladle the stew into shallow bowls.

Gabriella's Pot Roast

STRACOTTO DI MANZO ALLA GABRIELLA

1 boneless chuck roast, 2½ to 3 pounds

Kosher or sea salt

Freshly ground black pepper

2 tablespoons extra-virgin olive oil

1 tablespoon unsalted butter

1 large or 2 medium yellow onions, finely chopped (about 2 cups)

2 cloves garlic, lightly crushed with the flat side of a knife blade

2 carrots, peeled and finely chopped

2 ribs celery, trimmed and finely chopped

1½ teaspoons chopped fresh thyme

1 cup dry white wine

1 cup *Salsa Semplice di Pomodoro* (page 30) or best-quality commercial tomato sauce (see Cook's Note)

1 cup *Sostanzioso Brodo di Manzo* (page 25), *Brodo di Carne* (page 26), or water

Risotto Semplice (page 152), *Polenta* (page 154), or *Polenta di Castagne* (see variation, page 154) for serving

COOK'S NOTE:

If you have no tomato sauce on hand, you can substitute 1 cup drained, chopped canned tomatoes.

Turn any leftover sauce into a second meal by using it to dress hot cooked pasta—farfalle or a short, sturdy cut such as rigatoni is a good choice. Sprinkle generously with freshly grated *Parmigiano-Reggiano* cheese.

This is the pot roast of my childhood. I considered it a special occasion whenever my mother served it—which, no matter how often, was never often enough for me. Unlike a classic American pot roast, this version has no potatoes. The result is less starchy and more refined.

MAKES 6 MAIN-COURSE SERVINGS

Heat the oven to 325 degrees F.

Season the chuck roast with salt and pepper. In a Dutch oven or other heavy-bottomed pot with a lid, heat the olive oil and butter over medium-high heat. When the butter has melted and begins to sizzle, place the roast in the pot. Brown it on all sides, turning it every 3 to 4 minutes for even coloring. Remove the meat to a plate.

Reduce the heat to medium, add the onion, garlic, carrot, and celery, and sauté, stirring frequently, for about 10 minutes, or until the vegetables are tender and the onion is pale gold but not browned. Stir in the thyme, followed by the wine, tomato sauce, and the broth. Season with additional salt and pepper if you like.

Return the meat to the pot along with any juices that have accumulated on the plate. Bring the mixture to a simmer, cover, and place in the oven. Let the pot roast braise, turning the meat every 30 minutes, for about 2½ hours, or until it is fork-tender and the sauce is deliciously thick and red-brown.

Remove the meat from the sauce and let it sit for about 10 minutes before cutting it into thin slices. Arrange the slices on a serving platter and spoon some of the sauce over them (see Cook's Note). Or, if the meat is especially tender, you may use a fork to separate it into chunks and serve the stew in shallow bowls with some of the sauce spooned over. Serve with the risotto.

Artichoke Stew with Lettuce and Peas

STUFATO DI CARCIOFI CON LATTUGA E PISELLI

Juice of 2 lemons

4 to 5 cups water

4 large artichokes

2 tablespoons extra-virgin olive oil

1 tablespoon finely minced fatback or pancetta (optional)

1 clove garlic, passed through a garlic press

1 teaspoon kosher or sea salt

4 to 5 small sprigs fresh thyme

Freshly ground black pepper

1 cup shelled fresh or frozen English peas

1 heart romaine lettuce, washed, trimmed, and shredded

½ cup heavy cream, at room temperature

Risotto Semplice (page 152) for serving

Fresh English peas are hard to come by. They turn starchy soon after being picked, which is why you don't often see them in the produce aisle at the super-market. But if you have a pea patch or can otherwise get your hands on some garden-fresh peas, you may use them in place of the frozen ones in this recipe. Just be sure to add them to the pot a little bit sooner—about 5 minutes after you put in the artichokes—to give them enough time to cook properly.

MAKES 4 MAIN-COURSE SERVINGS

In a nonreactive bowl large enough to hold the trimmed artichokes, combine the lemon juice and water.

PREPARE THE ARTICHOKES:
Working with 1 artichoke at a time, cut off the stem flush with the base. Using a paring knife, cut off the base of the stem and then cut around the outside of the stem to remove the tough outer layer. Cut the stem in half lengthwise and put the trimmed stem halves in the lemon water to prevent them from discoloring. Pull off the tough, dark green outer leaves of the artichoke, bending the leaves back until they snap off at the base. Continue to snap off the leaves until you reach the more tender, lighter-colored leaves. With a sharp chef's knife or a serrated knife, cut about 1 inch off the top of the artichoke. Cut the artichoke in half lengthwise and, using a small, sturdy spoon, scrape out the fuzzy choke. Cut the halves lengthwise one more time; you will have quartered the artichoke. Put the artichoke quarters in the lemon water and repeat the trimming procedure with the remaining 3 artichokes.

TO MAKE THE STEW:
In a Dutch oven or other heavy-bottomed pot, heat the olive oil and fatback over medium heat. In a small bowl, mix together the garlic and salt to form a paste. When the oil is just starting to shimmer, add the paste to the pot, stirring well. Cook for a minute or two, or until the garlic releases its fragrance. Drain the artichokes, reserving ¾ cup of the lemon water, and add the artichokes to the pot along with the reserved water, thyme, and several grinds of pepper.

CONTINUED

Raise the heat to medium-high and bring to a boil. Reduce the heat to medium-low, cover, and simmer the stew for 15 to 20 minutes, or until the artichokes are somewhat tender but still a little firm when poked in the center with a knife. Uncover, raise the heat to medium, and cook until all but a few tablespoons of the liquid has evaporated.

Add the peas and cook, stirring, for 1 minute, or until they have lost their frosty sheen. Stir in the lettuce and the cream, reduce the heat once again to medium-low, and cook for 5 to 7 more minutes without boiling, or until the lettuce has wilted and the peas are just cooked through but still bright green.

Spoon the risotto into shallow bowls. Ladle the stew over the top.

BIETOLA CON LE PATATE

3 large yellow-fleshed potatoes such as Yukon gold, scrubbed clean

2 large bunches Swiss chard, washed and ends trimmed from stems (see Cook's Note)

⅓ cup extra-virgin olive oil

4 large cloves garlic, lightly crushed with the flat side of a knife blade

Kosher or sea salt

COOK'S NOTE:

Several kinds of chard, a member of the beet family, are available in supermarkets. The most common variety has crinkly, dark green leaves and pale green stems. Red chard is distinguished by its scarlet-veined leaves and scarlet-tinged stalks, while the increasingly popular rainbow chard includes a mix of stem colors, from magenta and orange to pale yellow and the standard green. For this recipe, I prefer to stick with the standard, as the colored varieties—particularly red—will stain the potatoes.

I have loved the earthy combination of Swiss chard and potatoes for as long as I can remember. There is nothing fancy about it; it is homey and satisfying. It is intended as a side dish and goes especially well with roast chicken or a frittata. But sometimes I just like to eat a big bowl of it, with bread on the side, and maybe a fried egg on top.

MAKES 4 TO 6 SIDE-DISH SERVINGS

In a pot, combine the potatoes with water to cover by 1 inch. Bring to a boil over medium-high heat and cook for about 20 minutes, or until the potatoes are tender. Drain and let cool. Peel the potatoes and cut into 2-inch chunks. Set aside.

Cut the stems from the leafy green chard leaves, and then cut the stems into 2-inch pieces. Stack the leaves, a few at a time, and cut them crosswise into 1-inch-wide strips.

In a sauté pan with a lid large enough to hold the potatoes and greens, heat the oil over medium heat. Add the garlic and sauté for about 2 minutes, or until the garlic releases its fragrance (do not let it brown). Add the chard stems and sauté, stirring every so often, for 5 to 7 minutes, or until they begin to soften. Stir in the chard leaves, tossing to coat with the oil. (You may have to add the leaves in several batches and wait for them to wilt before you add more.) Add the cooked potatoes and sprinkle with salt. Cover, reduce the heat to medium-low, and let the vegetables stew in the juices released from the greens, stirring occasionally, for about 20 minutes, or until the chard has turned dark and is completely tender.

Taste and adjust the seasoning with salt if needed. Spoon the chard and potatoes into a decorative serving bowl and serve hot.

CHAPTER 5

ESTATE
Recipes for Summer

125 Fiori di Zucca in
Brodo Estiva
Zucchini Blossoms in Summer
Broth

127 Pancotto con le Zucchine
alla Zia Gilda
Zia Gilda's Zucchini and
Bread Soup

128 Zuppa per Settembre
September Soup

130 Tubetti con Verdura Estiva
Tubetti with Summer Vegetables

131 Pasta e Ceci al Rosmarino
Pasta and Chickpeas with
Rosemary

132 Zuppetta di Farro
Spezzetato
Cracked Farro Soup

133 Zuppa di Cozze con
Peperoni Arrosti
Mussel Stew with Roasted
Peppers

134 Tonno e Cannellini in Salsa
Tuna and White Bean Stew

135 Spezzatino di Vitello con i
Peperoni
Veal and Pepper Stew

136 Polpettine Farcite in
Salsa Estiva
Olive-Stuffed Meatballs in
Light Tomato Sauce

139 Stufato di Pesce Spada
Overnight-Marinated
Swordfish Stew

140 Pollo alle Melanzane
Chicken with Eggplant

141 Rotolo di Manzo Farcito e
Brasato
Stuffed Beef Roll in Tomato
Sauce

144 Peperoni e Uova
Peppers and Eggs

145 Fagiolini all'Uccelletto
Green Beans Stewed
with Tomatoes

The return of grilling season does not mean the end of soup and stew season in my kitchen—far from it. Nor does my summer soup repertoire suddenly become limited to dainty, chilled cream-based soups. Italians generally don't like cold soups and, with a few exceptions, neither do I.

What I do like is taking advantage of summer's parade of racy vegetables to create endless combinations for vegetable soup, to be enjoyed hot, warm, or even at room temperature. In fact, in summer I hardly ever make the same soup twice. I much prefer to be guided by what's in the stalls at my local farmers' market, from eggplants in all shades of purple and even fiery orange to pole beans in deep burgundy or pale yellow.

August and September are when I try to get my fill of tomatoes and peppers because I know they will never taste as good as they do during those weeks. Together they are a luscious combination, whether paired in a stew with tender chunks of veal, in a rustic concoction of peppers and eggs, or puréed to a smooth soup.

Summer stews naturally tend to be lighter than their cold-weather cousins, and like Italian summer soups, they are delicious served hot or just warm. A savory stew of swordfish, cherry tomatoes, and briny purple olives is a welcome change from the usual fish kebabs. And while I love flank steak on the grill, there are some nights when nothing will do but rolled flank steak, stuffed with a savory filling of hard-boiled eggs and prosciutto and braised in tomato sauce to succulent perfection. On a late summer evening, when you can feel the air beginning to change, a slice of rolled flank steak enrobed in its rich, beef-infused sauce is nothing less than a slice of heaven.

FIORI DI ZUCCA IN BRODO ESTIVA

3 carrots, peeled and cut into fat coins or chunks

3 ribs celery, trimmed and cut crosswise into 2-inch pieces

2 yellow onions, each cut into 8 wedges

2 plum tomatoes, cored and cut into chunks

1 fennel bulb, trimmed and cut into 8 wedges

2 tablespoons extra-virgin olive oil

1 teaspoon kosher or sea salt

8 cups (2 quarts) water

⅓ cup fresh flat-leaf parsley leaves

¼ teaspoon black peppercorns (about 20)

1 cup coarsely chopped fresh basil

½ cup dry white wine

24 zucchini or other squash blossoms, gently rinsed and patted dry with paper towels (see Cook's Note)

8 slices *Crostini* (page 148)

Freshly grated *Parmigiano-Reggiano* cheese for serving

COOK'S NOTE:

Zucchini blossoms can be hard to come by unless you grow the squash plants in your garden, in which case you will have more than enough at your disposal. The blossoms are delicate and perishable and must be used the day they are picked, which is why you won't find them in most supermarkets. A growing number of farmers' markets do carry them, however, so look for them. Or, you might consider befriending someone who grows them. As you clean them, carefully pry them open from the top and check for any little bugs that may have taken up residence inside. Some cooks pull out the stamen inside each blossom, but I usually leave it in; either way is fine.

My original idea for this recipe was much more elaborate than the version here. It called for stuffing squash blossoms with a light cheese filling, frying the stuffed blossoms, and serving them in the broth. The batter, however, obscured the beautiful curves and the bright orange and pale green of the flowers. In the end, I decided to simplify things, so I skipped the stuffing and the batter and poached the blossoms. The result is this lovely, light soup, the perfect start to a summer dinner party.

MAKES 6 TO 8 FIRST-COURSE SERVINGS OR 4 MAIN-COURSE SERVINGS

Heat the oven to 450 degrees F.

Place the carrots, celery, onions, tomatoes, and fennel in a single layer in a large roasting pan. Drizzle with the olive oil and sprinkle with the salt, and then toss with a wooden spoon or spatula to coat the vegetables evenly with the oil and salt. Roast, turning the vegetables with a heat-proof rubber spatula or wooden spoon every 15 minutes, for 45 minutes, or until the vegetables are completely tender and well browned in places. Remove from the oven.

Tip the vegetables and their juices into a large saucepot and pour in the water. Add the parsley and peppercorns and bring to a boil over medium-high heat. Reduce the heat to medium-low, cover partially, and cook for 30 to 40 minutes, or until the broth is richly flavored. Add the basil and wine and simmer, uncovered, for an additional 10 minutes.

Remove the broth from the heat and let sit for 5 minutes. Using a fine-mesh sieve lined with damp paper towels or cheesecloth, strain the broth into a clean pot. Discard the solids.

Reheat the broth over medium heat just until it is simmering. Add the squash blossoms, taking care to handle them gently. Poach the blossoms for 5 minutes, or until they are just tender.

To serve, place 2 *crostini* in each of 4 shallow bowls. Ladle an equal amount of the broth and 6 blossoms into each bowl. To serve, sprinkle each bowl with a generous spoonful of the cheese.

3 tablespoons extra-virgin olive oil

1 tablespoon unsalted butter

1 small yellow onion, halved and thinly sliced

1 clove garlic, passed through a garlic press

1 teaspoon kosher or sea salt

3 zucchini, about 1 pound total weight, trimmed and thinly sliced

4 cups *Brodo di Pollo* (page 24), water, or best-quality canned low-sodium chicken broth

3 cups lightly toasted country bread cubes (see Cook's Note)

2 large eggs

1 cup freshly grated *Parmigiano-Reggiano* cheese

8 to 10 large fresh basil leaves, cut crosswise into fine strips (chiffonade)

Best-quality extra-virgin olive oil for serving

COOK'S NOTE:

To make the toasted bread cubes, cut the crusts off 4 slices Italian country bread, each 1 inch thick. Cut the slices into 1-inch cubes. You should have 3 lightly packed cups of bread cubes. Spread the cubes out on a rimmed baking sheet and bake in a 350°F oven for 15 to 20 minutes, or until lightly toasted.

You can prepare the soup through the addition and simmering of the bread cubes up to 4 hours ahead of time. Remove the soup from the heat and then reheat it to a simmer before adding the eggs and cheese and finishing the cooking.

Zia Gilda's Zucchini and Bread Soup

PANCOTTO CON LE ZUCCHINE ALLA ZIA GILDA

My mother's eldest sister, Gilda, never thought of herself as a talented cook, but the rest of us knew better. Among her specialties was this humble but delicious and wholesome soup of bread, zucchini, eggs, and cheese. I like it best served just warm.

MAKES 6 FIRST-COURSE SERVINGS OR 3 TO 4 MAIN-COURSE SERVINGS

In a Dutch oven or saucepot with a lid, heat 1 tablespoon of the olive oil and the butter over medium heat. Add the onion and sauté for 7 to 8 minutes, or until soft and translucent. In a small bowl, mix together the garlic and salt to form a paste and add the paste to the onion. Stir well and cook for about 1 minute, or until the garlic releases its fragrance. Stir in the zucchini and the remaining 2 tablespoons oil. Reduce the heat to medium-low and cook, stirring from time to time, for about 20 minutes, or until the zucchini slices are tender but still hold their shape.

Pour in the broth and raise the heat to medium-high. Bring the soup to a boil and add the bread cubes. Reduce the heat once again to medium-low and let the soup simmer gently, uncovered, for about 10 minutes (see Cook's Note).

Break the eggs into a bowl, add the cheese, and beat together lightly. Pour the egg mixture in a stream into the soup, and stir until the egg forms raggedy strands. Cook for 5 more minutes and then remove from the heat.

Stir in the basil and let the soup rest for 10 minutes. Ladle into shallow bowls and finish with a drizzle of your best olive oil.

September Soup
ZUPPA PER SETTEMBRE

1½ pounds plum tomatoes (about 9), cored, quartered lengthwise, and seeded

1 pound red bell peppers (about 3), trimmed, quartered lengthwise, and seeded

2 red or yellow onions, trimmed and each onion cut into 8 wedges

2 cloves garlic, quartered lengthwise

1 teaspoon kosher or sea salt

Freshly ground black pepper

1 teaspoon sweet Hungarian paprika

1 teaspoon finely chopped fresh thyme

6 large fresh basil leaves, cut crosswise into fine strips (chiffonade) or coarsely chopped

⅓ cup extra-virgin olive oil

2 cups *Brodo di Magro* (page 27), *Brodo di Pollo* (page 24), or best-quality canned low-sodium chicken broth

¼ cup heavy cream, at room temperature

Sourdough croutons (see *Dadini di Pane al Pepe* variation, page 150) for serving

COOK'S NOTE:
This soup is equally delicious chilled. Instead of garnishing with croutons, use finely diced green tomatoes, chopped black olives, or a dollop of mascarpone cheese or crème fraîche.

In September, the stalls at my local farmers' market in northern Virginia are brimming with tomatoes of all kinds and with fleshy, sweet bell peppers in red, yellow, orange, and purple. This soup brings out the best in both vegetables.

MAKES 6 FIRST-COURSE SERVINGS OR 3 TO 4 MAIN-COURSE SERVINGS

Heat the oven to 450 degrees F.

Place the tomatoes, bell peppers, onions, and garlic in a single layer in a large roasting pan. Sprinkle with the salt, pepper, paprika, thyme, and basil and drizzle with the olive oil. Toss with a wooden spoon or spatula to coat the vegetables evenly with the oil and seasonings. Roast, turning the vegetables with a heatproof rubber spatula or wooden spoon every 15 minutes, for 45 minutes, or until the vegetables are completely tender and well browned in places.

Remove from the oven and let cool for 10 to 15 minutes. In a blender or food processor, and working in 2 batches if necessary, purée the vegetables with the broth until smooth. Pass the purée through a fine-mesh sieve or a food mill fitted with the plate that has the smallest holes. This will eliminate bits of peel from the tomatoes and peppers.

Transfer the purée to a saucepan and reheat over low heat. Stir in the cream and heat the soup just until warmed through but not boiling.

Ladle the soup into shallow bowls and top with the croutons.

Tubetti with Summer Vegetables

TUBETTI CON VERDURA ESTIVA

1 small eggplant, about 8 ounces, trimmed and cut crosswise into ½-inch-thick slices

Kosher or sea salt

¼ cup extra-virgin olive oil

2 cloves garlic, lightly crushed with the flat side of a knife blade

1 small yellow onion, halved and thinly sliced

1 medium red potato, peeled and cut into ½-inch dice

1 medium zucchini or other summer squash, trimmed and cut into ½-inch dice

1 red or yellow bell pepper (or ½ each for more color), trimmed, seeded, and cut into ½-inch dice

Freshly ground black pepper

4 cups *Brodo di Magro* (page 27) or best-quality canned low-sodium vegetable broth, heated to a simmer

1 cup *tubetti, ditalini,* or small shell pasta

1 cup freshly grated *pecorino romano* cheese, plus some shavings for garnish

10 fresh basil leaves, cut crosswise into fine strips (chiffonade)

Best-quality extra-virgin olive oil for serving

COOK'S NOTE:
For fun, try a color-coordinated variation. For example, use yellow summer squash, yellow bell peppers, and roasted corn; or zucchini, green beans, spinach, and basil.

This is the perfect recipe for people who love to experiment in the kitchen. It gives you the opportunity to take advantage of the wonderful selection of high-summer vegetables, from pale purple eggplants and egg-shaped zucchini to red, yellow, orange, or deep purple peppers. And, unless you want to, you never have to make it the same way twice. I rarely do. Use the vegetables listed below as a guideline and take it from there (see Cook's Note).

MAKES 3 TO 4 MAIN-COURSE SERVINGS

Sprinkle the eggplant slices with a little salt and put them in a colander. Set a plate over the slices and weight it down with a heavy object. Let the eggplant slices sit for 30 minutes to release any bitter juices. Wipe the slices dry with a paper towel and cut them into ½-inch cubes. Set aside.

In a Dutch oven or other heavy-bottomed pot, heat the ¼ cup olive oil over medium heat. Add the garlic and onion and sauté for 3 to 4 minutes, or until the onion starts to soften. Stir in the eggplant, potato, zucchini, and bell pepper and season with black pepper. Cook the vegetables, stirring them every few minutes to keep them from sticking to the bottom of the pot, for 15 to 20 minutes, or until they are tender but still hold their shape.

Pour in the broth and raise the heat to medium-high. Bring the soup to a boil and stir in the pasta. Boil until it is al dente; the cooking time will vary depending on which pasta you use and the brand.

Remove from the heat and stir in the grated cheese and basil. Ladle the soup into a tureen or individual shallow bowls. Garnish each serving with the shaved cheese and a generous drizzle of your best olive oil.

Pasta with Chickpeas and Rosemary

PASTA E CECI AL ROSMARINO

3 cloves garlic, lightly crushed with the flat side of a knife blade

3 tablespoons extra-virgin olive oil

2 yellow onions, thinly sliced

1 tablespoon finely chopped fresh rosemary

1 can (28 ounces) whole tomatoes, coarsely crushed with a potato masher or fork, or 2 pounds fresh plum tomatoes (about 12), peeled, cored, seeded, and coarsely chopped (page 16)

1 can (15 ounces) chickpeas, rinsed and drained

2 cups *Brodo di Magro* (page 27), *Brodo di Pollo* (page 24), or best-quality canned low-sodium chicken broth

1 teaspoon Kosher or sea salt

Freshly ground black pepper

1½ cups short, sturdy pasta such as shells

Freshly grated *Parmigiano-Reggiano* or *pecorino romano* cheese for serving

COOK'S NOTE:
Pasta cooked in a thick soup takes longer to cook than pasta in water. Test for doneness by tasting.

My family does a lot of grilling in summer, which means at a certain point I get tired of it. That's when I make this soup. It's fast, satisfying, and convenient. In fact, you'll want to remember this soup on one of those evenings when you get home from work, bone tired and without a clue as to what to put on the table for dinner. For the sake of convenience, the recipe calls for canned tomatoes, but if you've got great tomatoes in your garden or from your farmers' market, by all means use them.

MAKES 6 TO 8 FIRST-COURSE SERVINGS OR 4 MAIN-COURSE SERVINGS

In a large Dutch oven or other heavy-bottomed pot, warm the garlic in the olive oil over medium heat. When the garlic is fragrant and just beginning to sizzle, add the onions and sauté, stirring, for 8 to 10 minutes, or until they have softened and are translucent but not browned. They should be sizzling, not screaming, so reduce the heat to medium-low if necessary. Sprinkle in the rosemary and mix well.

Pour the tomatoes into the pot. Bring the soup to a boil over medium heat and simmer for 10 minutes, or until the tomatoes have begun to break down but still have a lot of liquid. Do not simmer the tomatoes for longer or you'll end up with a pot of sauce.

Add the chickpeas, broth, salt, and several grinds of pepper and bring to a simmer. Turn off the heat and let the soup rest for 10 minutes or so to allow the flavors to mingle. In fact, you can leave it be until you're ready to cook the pasta.

To finish the soup, bring it to a boil over medium-high heat and pour in the pasta. Cover partially and cook, stirring from time to time to prevent the pasta from sticking to the bottom of the pot, for 15 to 20 minutes, or until the pasta is al dente (see Cook's Note). If the soup becomes too thick, add a splash more broth or a little water.

Taste and adjust the seasoning with salt and pepper. Ladle into deep bowls and serve, passing the freshly grated cheese at the table for sprinkling over the soup.

ZUPPETTA DI FARRO SPEZZETATO

2 cups pearled *farro*, rinsed and drained

¼ cup extra-virgin olive oil

1 yellow onion, finely chopped

1 clove garlic, passed through a garlic press

1 teaspoon kosher or sea salt

3 tablespoons tomato paste

8 cups (2 quarts) *Brodo di Magro* (page 27) or best-quality canned low-sodium vegetable broth, heated to a simmer

Generous pinch of red pepper flakes

Best-quality extra-virgin olive oil for serving

10 large fresh basil leaves, cut crosswise into fine strips (chiffonade)

Cracked farro resembles cracked bulgur wheat and has a nice chewy texture when cooked. It is not as easy to find as whole pearled farro, so you will probably need to treat pearled farro to a quick zap in the blender. (If you do find cracked farro, use 2 cups.) This soup is best served immediately. If left to sit, the farro will continue to absorb broth and soften. On the other hand, there is something to be said for a bowl of porridgy leftover farro soup, thinned out with a little broth and refreshed with a splash of good olive oil.

MAKES 6 TO 8 FIRST-COURSE SERVINGS OR 4 MAIN-COURSE SERVINGS

Place half of the *farro* in a blender and process for 30 to 45 seconds, or until it is coarsely chopped or "cracked." Repeat with the remaining *farro*.

In a Dutch oven or other heavy-bottomed pot, heat the olive oil over medium heat. Add the onion and sauté for 5 minutes, or until slightly softened. In a small bowl, mix together the garlic and salt to form a paste. Add the paste to the onion, stirring to incorporate it thoroughly. Stir in the *farro* and sauté for 3 to 4 minutes, or until the onion is translucent and the *farro* is thoroughly coated.

Dilute the tomato paste in 1 cup of the broth and add it to the pot. Pour in the rest of the broth and season with red pepper flakes. Raise the heat to medium-high and bring the soup to a boil. Reduce the heat to medium-low, cover partially, and simmer for about 40 minutes, or until the *farro* is tender but still pleasantly chewy.

Taste and adjust the seasoning with salt. Ladle the soup into shallow bowls and finish with a drizzle of your best olive oil and a sprinkle of basil.

Mussel Stew with Roasted Peppers

ZUPPA DI COZZE CON PEPERONI ARROSTI

Ingredients

2 red bell peppers

¼ cup extra-virgin olive oil

2 cloves garlic, minced

1 small yellow onion, halved and sliced paper-thin

2 small fresh red chili peppers, minced, or generous pinch of red pepper flakes

¾ pound plum tomatoes (about 4), peeled, cored, seeded, and coarsely chopped (page 16)

½ cup dry white wine

2 pounds small to medium mussels (about 6 dozen), thoroughly cleaned (page 16)

Kosher or sea salt

½ cup chopped fresh basil

4 to 6 slices *Bruschetta* (page 151)

Best-quality extra-virgin olive oil for serving

COOK'S NOTE:
This stew makes an excellent pasta sauce, too. As soon as the cooked mussels are cool enough to handle, remove them from their shells and stir them back into the sauce. Serve over cooked capellini.

Here, classic Neapolitan zuppa di cozze gets a makeover with the addition of roasted red sweet peppers and with basil rather than parsley, the traditional herb of choice. Farm-raised mussels are readily available year-round at fish markets and supermarket fish counters. They are often already debearded, making them much easier and faster to clean.

MAKES 4 TO 6 MAIN-COURSE SERVINGS

TO ROAST THE PEPPERS:
Heat the broiler. Put the bell peppers on a rimmed baking sheet and place under the broiler 4 inches from the heating element. Broil the peppers, using tongs to turn them every 3 to 4 minutes, until they are charred on all sides. Place the peppers in a bowl and cover tightly with plastic wrap. When they are cool enough to handle, remove the stems and cut the peppers in half, letting any liquid drain away. Peel the charred skin off the peppers with a small knife or your fingers, and remove any seeds and white pith from the inside. Cut the pepper halves lengthwise into narrow strips, and cut the strips into small dice. You should have about 1 packed cup total. Set aside.

TO MAKE THE STEW:
In a large Dutch oven or other heavy-bottomed pot with a lid, heat the olive oil over medium heat. Add the garlic, onion, and chili peppers and sauté, stirring frequently, for 4 minutes, or until the onion is just starting to soften. Stir in the diced roasted peppers and the tomatoes. Raise the heat to medium-high and pour in the wine. As soon as it begins to boil, add the mussels. Stir with a large spoon to coat the mussels with the sauce. Cover the pot and cook for 2 minutes. Uncover, stir, and taste for salt, adding a little if necessary. Re-cover and cook for another 2 to 3 minutes, or until all of the mussels have opened. Remove the pot from the heat and discard any mussels that failed to open. Stir in the basil.

Place a slice of *bruschetta* in each shallow soup bowl and ladle the mussels and sauce over the bread, dividing the mussels evenly among the bowls. Drizzle each serving with your best olive oil.

Tuna and White Bean Stew

TONNO E CANNELLINI IN SALSA

The mild flavor and meaty texture of white-fleshed albacore tuna are just right for this summer stew. There is no need to serve this piping hot, but be sure to have plenty of bruschetta on hand as an accompaniment.

MAKES 3 TO 4 MAIN-COURSE SERVINGS

2 cloves garlic, lightly crushed with the flat side of a knife blade

1 sprig fresh rosemary, about 5 inches long

3 tablespoons extra-virgin olive oil

1 pound albacore tuna steaks, cut into ¾-inch chunks (any bones discarded)

Kosher or sea salt

Freshly ground black pepper

1 red bell pepper, trimmed, seeded, and cut into small dice

1 can (15 ounces) *cannellini* beans, rinsed and drained

1 pound plum tomatoes (about 6), peeled, cored, seeded, and coarsely chopped (page 16)

2 to 4 Rizzoli brand *alici in salsa piccante* (page 18) or best-quality Italian anchovy fillets in olive oil, drained and chopped

Generous pinch of ground cayenne pepper

6 to 8 slices *Bruschetta* (page 151)

In a large sauté pan or skillet, warm the garlic and rosemary sprig in 2 tablespoons of the olive oil over medium heat. When the garlic begins to sizzle, add the tuna and increase the heat to medium-high. Season with a little salt and pepper and cook the tuna, tossing frequently, for no more than 5 minutes, or until it is lightly browned. Using tongs or a slotted spoon, remove the tuna to a bowl and set aside.

Add the remaining 1 tablespoon oil to the sauté pan and reduce the heat to medium. Stir in the bell pepper, *cannellini* beans, tomatoes, anchovy fillets, and cayenne pepper. Sauté for 10 to 15 minutes, or until the sauce thickens. Return the tuna to the pan and sauté for a few minutes more, or until the tuna is warmed through. The stew will be thick.

Taste and adjust the seasoning with salt and black pepper. Ladle the stew into shallow bowls and serve the *bruschetta* alongside.

Veal and Pepper Stew

SPEZZATINO DI VITELLO CON I PEPERONI

2 tablespoons extra-virgin olive oil

1 tablespoon unsalted butter

2 pounds boneless veal shoulder, cut into 1-inch cubes

1 yellow onion, finely chopped

3 or 4 bell peppers (1½ pounds), in a mixture of red, yellow, and orange, trimmed, seeded, and cut lengthwise into ½-inch-wide strips

Kosher or sea salt

Freshly ground black pepper

1 cup dry white wine

½ cup *Salsa Fresca di Pomodoro* (page 28), *Salsa Semplice di Pomodoro* (page 30), or best-quality commercial tomato sauce

2 teaspoons minced fresh basil

2 teaspoons minced fresh flat-leaf parsley

COOK'S NOTE:

This stew can be made ahead of time and refrigerated for up to 3 days or frozen for longer. In fact, I think the flavor improves if the stew is given the chance to sit for a while, even if it's just for a couple of hours off the heat on the same day you make it. This time allows the sauce to thicken and enriches the overall flavor of the mixture. If you do make it ahead of time, leave out the parsley and basil, but remember to add them just before serving.

Stewing veal is sometimes hard to find at a standard supermarket or even at a butcher shop, but you can usually ask the butcher at the market or the shop to order it for you.

Here, a red and golden pepper sauce and tender chunks of meat perfectly bridge the flavors and colors of summer and fall. Veal, lighter and milder in taste than beef, is the meat of choice here. In fact, I can hardly think of a better stew duet, at summer's end, than veal and peppers. The recipe can easily be doubled, which makes this a great dish for a dinner party. Serve with crusty fresh bread or Bruschetta (page 151) and with a green salad.

MAKES 4 MAIN-COURSE SERVINGS

In a large Dutch oven or other heavy-bottomed pot with a lid, heat the olive oil and butter over medium-high heat. When the oil is hot, brown the veal in 3 or 4 batches, taking care not to crowd the pot or the meat will steam rather than brown. Toss the meat cubes once or twice as they cook for even browning. Each batch should take about 5 minutes. As each batch is ready, use a slotted spoon to remove it to a shallow bowl. Repeat until all the meat is browned.

Add the onion and peppers to the pot and stir to combine thoroughly. Let the vegetables sizzle for about a minute as you toss them, then return the meat to the pot and season with salt and pepper. Pour in the wine and bring to a boil. Reduce the heat to medium and stir in the tomato sauce. Reduce the heat to low, cover, and simmer gently for about 1¼ hours, or until the veal is tender but not falling apart (check by piercing the meat with a fork; it should slide in with just a little resistance).

Uncover, increase the heat slightly, and simmer for another 20 minutes or so, or until the sauce has reduced and thickened. The peppers will become very soft and partially melt into the sauce. Remove from the heat.

Taste and adjust the seasoning with salt and pepper. Sprinkle with the basil and parsley. Ladle the stew into shallow bowls.

Olive-Stuffed Meatballs in Light Tomato Sauce

POLPETTINE FARCITE IN SALSA ESTIVA

FOR THE SAUCE

2 tablespoons extra-virgin olive oil

3 carrots, peeled and finely chopped

1 yellow onion, finely chopped

2 ribs celery, trimmed and finely chopped

2 cans (28 ounces each) whole tomatoes, coarsely crushed with a potato masher or fork, or 4 pounds fresh plum tomatoes (about 24), peeled, cored, seeded, and coarsely chopped (page 16)

1 teaspoon kosher or sea salt

¾ cup water

2 tablespoons unsalted butter

FOR THE MEATBALLS

2 cups fresh bread crumbs (see Cook's Note, page 100)

1 cup whole milk, heated to warm

8 ounces ground beef

8 ounces ground pork

8 ounces ground veal

2 eggs, lightly beaten

1 clove garlic, finely minced

3 tablespoons minced fresh flat-leaf parsley

3 tablespoons freshly grated *Parmigiano-Reggiano* cheese

3 tablespoons freshly grated *pecorino romano* cheese

1 teaspoon kosher or sea salt

Freshly ground black pepper

12 pitted large green olives such as Cerignola or Sicilian

The ancient city of Ascoli Piceno, high in the mountains of the Marche, is famous for its deep-fried meat-and-cheese-stuffed olives. One day I decided to try the recipe in reverse and came up with these savory olive-stuffed meatballs. You might be happy to know that they are not deep-fried, but rather stewed in a light, summery sauce of tomatoes and carrots. The gentle simmering produces a truly tender meatball, which in turn enriches the flavor of the sauce as it cooks.

MAKES 4 TO 6 MAIN-COURSE SERVINGS

TO MAKE THE SAUCE:

In a large saucepan, warm the olive oil over medium heat. Add the carrots, onion, and celery and sauté for 15 to 20 minutes, or until the vegetables are shiny and the carrots have begun to soften. Stir frequently to prevent the onion from browning; the onion should be pale gold, and the carrots should be bright orange.

Pour in the tomatoes and season with the salt. Bring the sauce to a boil, then reduce the heat to medium-low and simmer, uncovered, for about 30 minutes, or until the carrots are completely tender. Remove from the heat and let cool for 10 minutes.

In a food processor or blender, and working in 2 batches, purée the sauce and return it to the pot. Dilute the sauce with the water and stir in the butter. Reheat the sauce over medium-low heat while you make the meatballs, keeping it just below a simmer.

TO MAKE THE MEATBALLS:

In a small bowl, combine the bread crumbs and milk and let sit for 5 minutes. Squeeze out the excess milk and discard. Put all the meats in a large bowl and add the moistened bread crumbs, eggs, garlic, parsley, cheeses, salt, and several grinds of pepper. Divide the mixture into 12 equal portions. Dampen your hands with cold water and shape each portion into a large ball. As you shape each meatball, press an olive into the center, taking care that the olive is completely and evenly surrounded by the meat mixture. Keep your hands moistened with cold water to prevent the mixture from sticking to them.

COOK'S NOTE:

For an especially savory treat, fill each olive with a little prosciutto or salami, or with a piece of provolone, before slipping it into the center of a meatball. The meatballs can, of course, be served with spaghetti. Cook 1 pound spaghetti, dress with some of the sauce, and divide among 6 shallow bowls. Top each portion with 2 meatballs. Sprinkle with a little freshly grated *Parmigiano-Reggiano*.

TO COOK THE MEATBALLS:

Raise the heat under the sauce to medium to bring to a gentle simmer. Carefully immerse the meatballs in the sauce; they do not need to be completely covered by the sauce. If your pot is not large enough to hold all of the meatballs comfortably, cook them in 2 batches, or transfer half of the sauce to another saucepan and divide the meatballs between the 2 pans.

Cook the meatballs at a gentle simmer, carefully turning them from time to time, for 30 to 40 minutes, or until they are cooked through. Reduce the heat to medium-low if the sauce is bubbling too vigorously; the meatballs are delicate and should stew slowly and gently.

Spoon the meatballs into shallow bowls, dividing them evenly. Spoon the sauce over the top.

STUFATO DI PESCE SPADA

1 swordfish steak (2 pounds), about 4 inches thick

   Kosher or sea salt

   Freshly ground black pepper

1 large or 2 medium yellow onions, halved and thinly sliced

12 ounces cherry tomatoes, stems removed, halved lengthwise

5 cloves garlic, lightly crushed with the flat side of a knife blade

1 cup pitted Gaeta or Kalamata olives

5 fresh bay leaves

1 rounded tablespoon minced fresh oregano

¾ cup extra-virgin olive oil

I adapted this recipe from one that I came across in an old issue of La Cucina Italiana, Italy's premier cooking magazine. My mother was a subscriber for many years, and one of my favorite pastimes is to flip through issues published in the 1960s, 1970s, and 1980s, in search of forgotten recipes such as this one. If you are used to tough, overgrilled swordfish steaks or kebabs, you are in for a treat. Here, a single large piece of fish is smothered with onions, tomatoes, olives, and herbs, covered, and left to marinate at length in the refrigerator. It is then slowly and gently simmered on the stove top, with no stirring at all. Cooked this way, the fish is mild, tender, and succulent, its brothy sauce infused with the perfume of bay leaf and oregano and the briny tang of the olives. Have a basket of crusty fresh bread or of Bruschetta (page 151) on the table for soaking up the juices.

MAKES 6 TO 8 MAIN-COURSE SERVINGS

Place the swordfish in a Dutch oven or other heavy-bottomed pot with a lid. It should fit comfortably but snugly. Season the fish generously on all sides with salt and pepper. Cover the fish with the onion, tomatoes, garlic, olives, bay leaves, and oregano. Drizzle the olive oil over everything, cover, and refrigerate overnight.

To cook the fish, remove the pot from the refrigerator and let it stand at room temperature for 45 to 60 minutes. Place the pot on the stove top over low heat and cook, covered, for 1 hour and 10 minutes or slightly longer, or until the fish is cooked through.

Discard the bay leaves. Using a large serving spoon, scoop out chunks of fish into shallow bowls. Spoon the broth, onion, tomatoes, and olives over the fish.

Chicken with Eggplant
POLLO ALLE MELANZANE

2 small purple Italian eggplants, about 1 pound total weight, trimmed and cut crosswise into ½-inch-thick slices

Kosher or sea salt

1 chicken, 4 pounds, cut into 10 serving pieces

Freshly ground black pepper

1 tablespoon extra-virgin olive oil

2 cloves garlic, lightly crushed with the flat side of a knife blade

1 small yellow onion, cut into small dice

12 ounces cherry tomatoes, stems removed, halved lengthwise

½ cup *Brodo di Pollo* (page 24) or best-quality canned low-sodium chicken broth

¾ cup pitted Gaeta or Kalamata olives, cut into large pieces

1 tablespoon balsamic vinegar

2 teaspoons finely chopped fresh basil

1 teaspoon finely chopped fresh flat-leaf parsley

COOK'S NOTE:
A simple potato salad of boiled and sliced russet potatoes, sprinkled with parsley, chives, and salt and dressed with good extra-virgin olive oil, makes a nice side dish to the robustly flavored chicken.

This summery stew has its origins in my local Thai restaurant, believe it or not, where spicy chicken with eggplant is one of my favorite dishes. The silky texture of the cooked eggplant gives the chicken a touch of elegance. Instead of chili peppers and fish sauce, I use briny purple olives and a splash of balsamic vinegar to punch up the flavors.

MAKES 4 MAIN-COURSE SERVINGS

Sprinkle the eggplant slices with a little salt and put them in a colander. Set a plate over the slices and weight it down with a heavy object. Let the eggplant slices sit for 30 minutes to release any bitter juices. Wipe the slices dry with a paper towel and cut them into quarters. Set aside.

Season the chicken lightly with salt and pepper. In a Dutch oven or high-sided sauté pan, heat the olive oil over medium-high heat. When the oil is hot, arrange half of the chicken pieces, skin side down, in the pot and let them brown for 4 to 5 minutes, or until the skin is a deep gold. Turn and cook for about 4 minutes on the other side, until browned. Remove the chicken to a large plate. Repeat with the remaining chicken pieces and remove them to the plate as well.

Reduce the heat to medium and add the garlic and onion to the pot. Sauté, stirring occasionally, for about 5 minutes, or until the onion is shiny and just beginning to soften. Add the eggplant pieces and stir to coat them thoroughly with the onion. Cook, stirring occasionally, for 5 minutes, or until the eggplant is slightly softened. Stir in the tomatoes and broth. Return the chicken to the pot and spoon some of the vegetables over the pieces. Reduce the heat to medium-low, cover, and cook the chicken at a steady but gentle simmer, reducing the heat to low if necessary, for 30 to 40 minutes, or until the chicken is cooked through and the meat comes easily off the bone.

Stir in the olives and vinegar. Raise the heat to medium and cook, uncovered, for 5 more minutes. Remove from the heat and sprinkle in the basil and parsley. Serve either in shallow bowls or on dinner plates.

Stuffed Beef Roll in Tomato Sauce

ROTOLO DI MANZO FARCITO E BRASATO

1 flank steak (1½ pounds), butterflied and pounded ¼ to ½ inch thick (see Cook's Note)

4 tablespoons extra-virgin olive oil

Kosher or sea salt

Freshly ground black pepper

½ cup fine dried bread crumbs

1 cup freshly grated *pecorino romano* cheese

2 cloves garlic, passed through a garlic press

2 tablespoons chopped mixed fresh herbs such as flat-leaf parsley, rosemary, marjoram, oregano, and thyme

2 ounces *prosciutto di Parma*, cut crosswise into narrow ribbons

3 hard-boiled eggs, peeled

½ cup dry white wine

3½ cups *Salsa Fresca di Pomodoro* (page 28) or *Salsa Semplice di Pomodoro* (page 30), diluted with ½ cup water and heated to a simmer

This has to be the ultimate summer comfort food—rolled flank steak stuffed with prosciutto, cheese, eggs, and bread crumbs and stewed in tomato sauce. It's visually appealing, too: each slice is a spiral of meat and stuffing with a sliver of yellow-and-white egg at its center. You can serve the roll hot, tepid, or even cold. Leftover slices make a great sandwich filling, while leftover sauce is perfect for dressing pasta.

MAKES 6 MAIN-COURSE SERVINGS

Lay the flank steak flat, cut side up, on a work surface and drizzle with 1 tablespoon of the olive oil. Rub the oil into the meat with your fingers. Sprinkle a little salt and a few grinds of pepper over the meat.

TO MAKE THE STUFFING:
In a small bowl, combine the bread crumbs, cheese, garlic, herbs, and prosciutto and mix thoroughly with your fingers. Drizzle in 2 tablespoons of the olive oil and mix again by hand until the oil is fully incorporated into the stuffing.

Firmly pat the stuffing onto the surface of the steak, leaving about a ½-inch border all around the edge. Now comes the tricky part: Line up the 3 eggs end to end along one short end of the steak, placing them about 1 inch in from the edge. Bring the edge of the meat up over the eggs and carefully roll the meat up around the eggs as tightly as you can, continuing until the entire steak has been rolled into a cylinder (see Cook's Note). Tie the roll securely with kitchen string at 3 or 4 evenly spaced intervals and season the outside of the roll with additional salt and pepper.

In a Dutch oven or other heavy-bottomed pot large enough to hold the roll, heat the remaining 1 tablespoon oil over medium heat. When the oil is hot, add the meat roll and sear on all sides, allowing 3 to 4 minutes on each side and turning the roll 3 or 4 times so that it is well browned all over. Remove the *rotolo* to a plate.

CONTINUED

COOK'S NOTE:

To butterfly the flank steak, lay it out in front of you on a work surface. Using a sharp knife and holding it parallel to the work surface, cut through the center of the meat, starting at the thin end and working your way toward the thicker end. Do not cut completely through, but stop about ½ inch from the end. You should now be able to open the flank steak up like a book. Place butterflied steak between 2 sheets of waxed paper and pound it firmly with a meat pounder until it is between ¼ and ½ inch thick. Try to get it as thin and as uniform as possible without tearing it. The alternative to all this work, of course, is to take the easy way out (like I do): ask your butcher or someone in the meat department of your supermarket to do the butterflying and pounding for you.

For a somewhat easier version of the *rotolo*, chop the eggs and sprinkle them over the filling before rolling the meat. The end result won't be quite as dramatic, but it will be just as delicious.

Increase the heat to medium-high, pour in the wine, and deglaze the pot, using a wooden spatula to scrape up any browned bits from the bottom. Let the wine evaporate for a minute or two, and then stir in the tomato sauce. Return the meat to the pot, rolling it around to coat it in the sauce. Bring to a boil, reduce the heat to low, cover, and simmer, turning every 30 minutes, for 1½ hours, or until the meat is fork-tender but still firm enough to slice without shredding. Remove the pot from the heat and let the *rotolo* sit in the sauce for about 10 minutes.

Remove the *rotolo* from the sauce to a cutting board and cut into ½-inch-thick slices. Meanwhile, gently reheat the sauce if it has cooled. Arrange the meat on a large serving platter and spoon some of the sauce over it. Pass a gravy boat with additional sauce at the table.

PEPERONI E UOVA

2 cloves garlic, lightly crushed with the flat side of a knife blade

¼ cup extra-virgin olive oil

1 large red bell pepper, trimmed, seeded, and cut lengthwise into ½-inch-wide strips

1 large yellow bell pepper, trimmed, seeded, and cut lengthwise into ½-inch-wide strips

3 plum tomatoes, peeled, cored, seeded, and coarsely chopped (page 16)

10 large fresh basil leaves, cut crosswise into fine strips (chiffonade)

Kosher or sea salt

¼ teaspoon sweet Hungarian paprika

Generous pinch of ground cayenne pepper

2 large eggs

½ cup freshly grated *pecorino romano* cheese

2 large slices *Bruschetta* (page 151)

I couldn't live without peppers and eggs, whether fried, scrambled into a frittata, or cooked up into this marvelous summer stew. The eggs are stirred in at the last minute, and the faster you stir, the creamier the stew will be. All you need to make a simple supper are thick slices of bruschetta and a glass of wine. For a more substantial dinner, serve the stew alongside grilled sausages.

MAKES 2 MAIN-COURSE SERVINGS

In a large sauté pan with a lid, warm the garlic in the olive oil over medium heat just until it begins to sizzle and release its fragrance, about 2 minutes. Do not let it brown. Add the peppers, stirring to coat them thoroughly with the oil. Reduce the heat to medium-low, cover partially, and simmer gently, stirring every so often and reducing the heat to low if necessary to prevent the peppers from scorching, for 30 minutes, or until the peppers are tender.

Uncover and stir in the tomatoes, basil, ½ teaspoon salt, paprika, and cayenne pepper. Continue to cook, uncovered, at a gentle simmer over low to medium-low heat for 15 minutes, or until the tomatoes are cooked and the stew has thickened.

In a small bowl, beat the eggs with ¼ cup of the cheese and a pinch of salt. Pour the eggs into the stew and stir vigorously with a wooden spoon or heatproof rubber spatula for about 3 minutes, or until the eggs are cooked and the mixture is creamy.

Place a slice of *bruschetta* into each of 2 shallow bowls and spoon the stew over the bread. Sprinkle with the remaining ¼ cup cheese, dividing it evenly.

3 tablespoons extra-virgin olive oil

1 clove garlic, minced

⅓ cup finely diced red onion

1 pound green beans, preferably romano beans (see Cook's Note), trimmed and snapped or cut into 1-inch pieces

2 large tomatoes, peeled, cored, seeded, and chopped (2½ to 2⅔ cups)

Kosher or sea salt

½ teaspoon ground cayenne pepper

1 tablespoon chopped fresh basil

COOK'S NOTE:
Romano beans are an Italian variety of green bean distinguished by their smooth, flat pods and pale green hue. You can find them in the summer at well-stocked supermarkets, Italian groceries, and farmers' markets.

Halloumi cheese, which originated in Cyprus, is usually made from goat's milk, or a mixture of goat's and sheep's milk, and a touch of mint. It is salty and mildly tangy, with a firm, slightly spongy texture. One of its most appealing features is that it can be cut into slices and grilled (or fried in oil or butter for that matter) without melting all over the place.

Green Beans Stewed with Tomatoes

FAGIOLINI ALL'UCCELLETTO

Meaty romano beans, with their broad, green pods and earthy flavor, are simmered to tenderness in fresh tomato sauce, or as the Italians say, all'uccelletto— in the manner of small game birds. This stew goes especially well with chicken cutlets, grilled lamb chops, or thick slices of grilled halloumi cheese (see Cook's Note). Serve with crusty Italian country bread for sopping up the sauce.

MAKES 4 SIDE-DISH SERVINGS

In a high-sided sauté pan with a lid, heat the olive oil over medium heat. Add the garlic and onion and sauté, stirring, for 5 to 7 minutes, or until the onion has softened and is translucent. Add the beans and sauté, stirring, for 2 minutes. Pour in the tomatoes and season with a little salt and the cayenne pepper. Reduce the heat to medium-low, cover, and simmer for 20 to 25 minutes, or until the beans are tender but not mushy.

Uncover, raise the heat to medium-high, and cook for 5 more minutes, or until the sauce has thickened. Remove to a serving bowl and scatter the basil over the top.

CHAPTER 6

ACCOMPANIMENTS
Perfect Partners and
Four Perfect Endings

148 Crostini
Toasted Bread Slices

149 Crostoni al Pecorino
Large Toasted Bread Slices with
Pecorino

150 Dadini di Pane al Pepe
Black Pepper Croutons

151 Bruschetta
Garlic-Rubbed Grilled Bread

152 Risotto Semplice
Simple Risotto

154 Polenta

FOUR SEASONAL
CROSTATE

156 Pasta Frolla
Pastry Dough

157 Crostata di Mele
Apple Tart

159 Crostata di Marmellata
Jam Tart

160 Crostata di Ricotta
Ricotta Cheese Tart

161 Crostata di Albicocche
e Amarene
Apricot and Sour Cherry Tart

Toasted Bread Slices
CROSTINI

½ thin baguette or *ficelle*

Extra-virgin olive oil for brushing

MAKES ABOUT 20 SLICES

Heat the oven to 375 degrees F. Cut the bread into ½-inch-thick slices and brush the slices on both sides with a little olive oil. Arrange the slices on a rimmed baking sheet.

Place the baking sheet in the oven and toast the bread slices for 7 to 8 minutes, or until they are golden around the edge and pale gold in the center. Turn the slices over and continue to toast for an additional 5 minutes, or until lightly browned on both sides. Remove from the oven and let the toasts cool to room temperature.

Store the toast slices in a large zipper-lock plastic bag at room temperature until ready to use.

CROSTINI AL PEPE (BLACK PEPPER CROSTINI) VARIATION

Follow the directions for *Crostini*, but grind a generous amount of black pepper over one side of the bread slices before toasting in the oven.

Large Toasted Bread Slices with Pecorino

CROSTONI AL PECORINO

8 slices Italian country bread, each cut ½ inch thick on the diagonal

2 tablespoons extra-virgin olive oil

8 tablespoons freshly grated *pecorino romano* cheese

Freshly ground black pepper

Crostoni are simply crostini made with larger slices of bread. They can be toasted in the oven or, as in this case, run under the broiler to melt and brown the cheese.

MAKES 8 SLICES

Heat the broiler.

Brush the top side of each bread slice with a little of the olive oil and place on a rimmed baking sheet. Top each slice evenly with 1 tablespoon of the cheese and a few grinds of pepper.

Place the baking sheet under the broiler about 4 inches from the heating element and broil the bread slices for 2 minutes, or until the edges of the bread slices are browned and the cheese topping is melted and pale gold. Serve hot or warm.

Black Pepper Croutons

DADINI DI PANE AL PEPE

4 cups cubed Italian country bread
(½-inch cubes)

3 tablespoons extra-virgin olive oil

½ teaspoon kosher or sea salt, or to taste
Freshly ground black pepper

Freshly ground pepper gives these croutons extra zest. Add them to hearty soups just before serving. They can be made in advance and stored in an airtight container in the refrigerator for up to a week. Just remember to bring them to room temperature before you use them.

MAKES 4 CUPS

Heat the oven to 400 degrees F.

Spread the bread cubes on a rimmed baking sheet and drizzle the olive oil over them. Toss well with a wooden spoon. Sprinkle on the salt and a liberal amount of pepper, toss again, and spread into a single layer.

Place the baking sheet in the oven and toast the croutons, stirring them once at the midpoint, for 15 to 20 minutes, or until they are evenly browned and crisp. Remove from the oven and let cool before storing.

VARIATIONS
For whole-wheat croutons, omit the pepper and use whole-wheat bread. For sourdough croutons, omit the pepper and use sourdough bread.

Garlic-Rubbed Grilled Bread

BRUSCHETTA

½ cup extra-virgin olive oil

1 large clove garlic, passed through a garlic press

6 to 8 slices Italian country bread, each ½ to ¾ inch thick

COOK'S NOTE:
Bruschetta can also be prepared on a charcoal or gas grill. Lightly brush both sides of each bread slice with the garlic oil and grill, turning once, to brown both sides.

Bruschetta can be used in the same way as crostini. A soup or stew can be ladled over the bread, or the bread can be served on the side. Bruschetta goes particularly well with seafood stews.

MAKES 6 TO 8 SLICES

Heat the broiler.

In a small bowl, mix together the oil and garlic and let sit for 10 minutes. Brush the garlic oil on one side of each bread slice, and arrange the slices, oiled side up, on a rimmed baking sheet.

Broil the bread slices for 1 to 2 minutes, or until the slices are slightly charred around the edges and golden in the middle. Serve hot or warm.

Simple Risotto
RISOTTO SEMPLICE

3 tablespoons unsalted butter

1 tablespoon extra-virgin olive oil

1 small yellow onion, finely chopped

2 cups Arborio or other risotto rice

About 6 cups *Brodo di Pollo* (page 24), *Brodo di Carne* (page 26), *Brodo di Magro* (page 27), or best-quality canned low-sodium chicken broth, heated to a simmer

Kosher or sea salt

Freshly ground black pepper

¾ cup freshly grated *Parmigiano-Reggiano* cheese

The fact that Arborio, the pearly short-grain rice used to make risotto, is available in supermarkets across the country is a testament to how well-loved this classic Italian dish has become. In fact, some shoppers now have a choice between Arborio and two other varieties of good risotto rice, Carnaroli and Vialone Nano. This basic risotto goes well with many of the stews in this book, but I especially recommend it as a side to Pollo Stufato con Trebbiano (page 83) and Stufato di Carciofi con Lattuga e Piselli (page 117).

MAKES 6 SERVINGS

In a Dutch oven or other heavy-bottomed pot, heat 1 tablespoon of the butter and the olive oil over medium heat. Add the onion and sauté for 7 to 8 minutes, or until it has softened and is translucent. Stir in the rice with a wooden spoon and mix well to coat the kernels thoroughly with the butter and oil. Cook, stirring often, for a minute or two, or until the rice is shiny and translucent.

Stir in ½ cup of the hot broth. Continue to stir well until the broth has been absorbed. Keep adding the hot broth, ½ cup at a time, stirring constantly until it is absorbed before adding more. Taste the rice for doneness after 20 to 25 minutes of cooking; it should be creamy and tender but still a little firm at the center of each kernel. When it has reached that stage, stir in one last splash of hot broth and season with salt and pepper. (You may not need all the broth.)

Add the remaining 2 tablespoons butter and the cheese and stir to combine thoroughly, then serve.

RISOTTO ALLO ZAFFERANO (SAFFRON RISOTTO) VARIATION
Dilute ½ teaspoon finely chopped saffron threads in ½ cup of the hot broth. Stir this mixture into the risotto halfway through cooking. This golden risotto is the perfect partner for *Osso Buco in Salsa Bruna* (page 88).

POLENTA

7 cups water

1 teaspoon kosher or sea salt

1½ cups polenta

3 tablespoons unsalted butter

¾ cup freshly grated *Parmigiano-Reggiano* cheese (optional)

Polenta is a soul-satisfying alternative to pasta, potatoes, or bread. It goes well with many of the stew recipes in the book, especially Costate di Maiale in Salsa di Pomodoro e Porcini (page 86) and Pollo in Salsa Piccante (page 55).

MAKES 4 TO 6 SERVINGS

In a heavy-bottomed saucepan, combine the water and 1 teaspoon salt and bring to a boil over medium-high heat. Very carefully sprinkle in the polenta in a slow, steady stream, stirring continuously with a wire whisk as you add it. When all the polenta has been mixed with the water, reduce the heat to medium and continue to cook the polenta, stirring frequently with a wooden spoon, for 40 to 45 minutes, or until it is very thick and comes away cleanly from the sides and bottom of the pan.

Add the butter and the cheese, if using, and stir vigorously until the butter is melted and well incorporated into the polenta. Taste and adjust the seasoning with salt if needed.

You can serve polenta in a variety of ways: Spoon it into shallow bowls and ladle stew over the top, or pour it into a decorative serving bowl or casserole, dot with additional butter, and sprinkle with freshly grated *Parmigiano-Reggiano* cheese. Or, spread it out into a circle or a rectangular slab, let it cool, and then cut it into wedges, squares, or rectangles and grill, fry, or bake it.

POLENTA DI CASTAGNE (CHESTNUT POLENTA) AND
POLENTA DI FRUMENTINO (BUCKWHEAT POLENTA) VARIATIONS

Here are two delicious variations on basic polenta. For chestnut polenta, substitute ¾ cup chestnut flour for half the cornmeal; for buckwheat polenta, substitute ¾ cup buckwheat flour for half the cornmeal. In both cases, mix the flour with the cornmeal before adding it to the boiling salted water. Cook as directed and stir in shredded Fontina cheese rather than *Parmigiano-Reggiano* at the end of cooking.

Polenta can also be made by substituting chicken broth (*Brodo di Pollo*, page 24) for the salted water. Or, for creamy polenta, substitute 3½ cups whole milk for half of the water. Cook as directed.

FOUR SEASONAL *CROSTATE*

A *crostata* is a classic Italian dessert tart. The shell is made from a rich, shortbreadlike pastry called *pasta frolla*, and the filling can be anything from jam or fresh fruit to pastry cream or Nutella, the chocolate-hazelnut spread favored by Italian children. My favorite *crostate* are the plainest ones, without glazes or fancy tropical fruits. They are beautifully rustic in appearance, often with a golden lattice-top crust, and they make a perfect ending to a comforting dinner of soup or stew. You can bake a *crostata* in almost any kind of shallow baking vessel, from a pie dish or a fluted tart pan with a removable bottom to a jelly roll pan or a rimmed pizza pan. I find a tart pan to be the most convenient because the *crostata* is easily removed once it has cooled.

Following are the recipes for *pasta frolla* and four fillings, one for each season. I encourage you to try these, but also to experiment with your own fillings, whether a favorite marmalade, berries, fresh figs, or custard.

Pastry Dough

PASTA FROLLA

3 cups unbleached all-purpose flour

1 cup confectioners' sugar

¼ teaspoon fine sea salt or table salt

Grated zest of 1 lemon

1 cup (½ pound) cold unsalted butter, cut into ½-inch cubes

1 large whole egg

2 large egg yolks

Tender pasta frolla can be tough to work with. It is buttery and tends to tear easily. But it is also easy to patch if it does tear. I promise you that you will get more adept at handling it each time you make it. Be sure to chill the dough thoroughly after mixing it for at least 1 hour, or as long as overnight is fine. If refrigerated overnight, remove the dough from the refrigerator about 45 minutes before rolling it out, enough time for the butter to soften slightly so that the dough is pliable. Use a lightly floured surface to roll out the dough and do not overwork it; too much flour and handling will yield a tough crust.

MAKES ENOUGH DOUGH FOR ONE 9-INCH OR 10-INCH LATTICE-TOP TART

This recipe yields slightly more dough than what you will need to make a 9-inch lattice-top crust. I find it is easier to roll out and fit the dough in the tart pan if you have a little extra to work with. Don't discard the scraps—they make delicious butter cookies. Just gather them together, reroll them, and cut into shapes with a cookie cutter. Bake the cookies in a 350 degree F oven for 15 to 20 minutes, or until they are lightly browned.

Put the flour, sugar, salt, and lemon zest in the work bowl of a food processor fitted with a metal blade. Pulse briefly to combine the ingredients. Distribute the butter around the bowl and pulse until the mixture is crumbly. Add the whole egg and egg yolks and process until the mixture just begins to clump together in the work bowl.

Turn the dough out onto a lightly floured work surface and pat it together into one solid piece; it does not have to be completely smooth. Without overworking it, shape the dough into a disk, patting rather than kneading it. Wrap tightly in plastic and refrigerate for at least 1 hour, or until well chilled.

156

Apple Tart

CROSTATA DI MELE

FOR THE TART SHELL

1 batch *Pasta Frolla* (facing page), slightly cooler than room temperature

Unbleached all-purpose flour for dusting work surface

FOR THE FILLING

6 sweet-tart apples, preferably at least two varieties, peeled, cored, and cut into ½-inch dice (about 7 cups)

3 tablespoons unsalted butter

½ cup granulated sugar

Juice of ½ lemon

Confectioners' sugar for garnish (optional)

For this tart, I like to use a mix of apple varieties to create a complex flavor. Among my favorites are Stayman, McIntosh, Suncrisp, and Albemarle Pippin, an apple that was favored by Thomas Jefferson.

MAKES ONE 9-INCH LATTICE-TOP TART

TO MAKE THE TART SHELL:

Cut the dough disk into 2 portions, one slightly larger than the other. Rewrap the smaller portion and set aside. On a lightly floured surface, roll out the larger portion into an 11-inch round about ⅛ inch thick or slightly thicker. Carefully wrap the dough around the rolling pin and drape it over a 9-inch fluted tart pan with a removable bottom. Gently press the dough into the bottom and up the sides of the pan. Use the rolling pin or the flat of your hand to press around the perimeter of the pan to cut off any excess dough. Put the lined tart pan in the refrigerator to chill for 30 minutes.

TO MAKE THE FILLING:

In a heavy-bottomed saucepan, combine the apples, butter, granulated sugar, and lemon juice and bring to a simmer over medium-high heat, stirring to prevent scorching. Cook, stirring frequently, for about 15 minutes, or until the apples are tender and the mixture has thickened. Remove from the heat and let cool to room temperature.

Heat the oven to 350 degrees F.

ASSEMBLE AND BAKE THE TART:

Remove the tart shell from the refrigerator. Spoon the cooled filling into the shell and smooth it with a rubber spatula. Roll out the remaining dough portion into a 10-inch round about ⅛ inch thick or slightly thicker, and cut it into ¾-inch-wide strips with a fluted pastry wheel. Carefully place the strips over the filled tart shell in a lattice pattern, gently pressing the ends of the strips into the sides of the tart shell.

Bake the *crostata* for 30 to 40 minutes, or until the crust is golden. Remove the *crostata* from the oven and place it on a wire rack to cool for 20 minutes, or until cool enough to handle. Remove the rim of the tart pan and let the *crostata* cool completely on the rack before transferring it to a decorative serving platter. Dust with confectioners' sugar if you like.

Jam Tart

CROSTATA DI MARMELLATA

FOR THE TART SHELL

1 batch *Pasta Frolla* (page 156), slightly cooler than room temperature

Unbleached all-purpose flour for dusting work surface

FOR THE FILLING

1 cup blackberry or other fruit preserves

Confectioners' sugar for garnish (optional)

I like the contrast of deep blackberry preserves against the golden lattice of the baked crostata, but just about any type of preserves will make a lovely tart, so use your favorite. If you are lucky enough to have any tart left over, enjoy it for breakfast with a frothy cup of cappuccino.

MAKES ONE 9-INCH LATTICE-TOP TART

TO MAKE THE TART SHELL:

Cut the dough disk into 2 portions, one slightly larger than the other. Rewrap the smaller portion and set aside. On a lightly floured surface, roll out the larger portion into an 11-inch round about $\frac{1}{8}$ inch thick or slightly thicker. Carefully wrap the dough around the rolling pin and drape it over a 9-inch fluted tart pan with a removable bottom. Gently press the dough into the bottom and up the sides of the pan. Use the rolling pin or the flat of your hand to press around the perimeter of the pan to cut off any excess dough. Put the lined tart pan in the refrigerator to chill for 30 minutes.

TO MAKE THE FILLING:

In a small saucepan, warm the jam over medium-low heat for about 5 minutes, or until it is slightly loosened. Remove from heat and let cool to room temperature.

Heat the oven to 350 degrees F.

ASSEMBLE AND BAKE THE TART:

Remove the tart shell from the refrigerator. Spoon the cooled jam into the shell and smooth it with a rubber spatula. Roll out the remaining dough portion into a 10-inch round about $\frac{1}{8}$ inch thick or slightly thicker, and cut it into $\frac{3}{4}$-inch-wide strips with a fluted pastry wheel. Carefully place the strips over the filled tart shell in a lattice pattern, gently pressing the ends of the strips into the sides of the tart shell.

Bake the *crostata* for 30 to 40 minutes, or until the crust is golden. Remove the *crostata* from the oven and place it on a wire rack to cool for 20 minutes, or until cool enough to handle. Remove the rim of the tart pan and let the *crostata* cool completely on the rack before transferring it to a decorative serving platter. Dust with confectioners' sugar if you like.

Ricotta Cheese Tart
CROSTATA DI RICOTTA

FOR THE TART SHELL

1 batch *Pasta Frolla* (page 156), slightly cooler than room temperature

Unbleached all-purpose flour for dusting work surface

FOR THE FILLING

1 pound fresh ricotta cheese

1 large whole egg

2 large egg yolks

½ cup confectioners' sugar

½ teaspoon pure vanilla extract

¼ teaspoon ground cinnamon

Confectioners' sugar for garnish (optional)

Please don't settle for the bland, gritty, mass-produced ricotta cheese sold in plastic tubs at the supermarket to make this tart or you will be disappointed. You can buy good fresh ricotta at many well-stocked supermarkets, gourmet grocery stores, cheese shops, and Italian delicatessens. It is sometimes labeled "hand-dipped" and has a light, yet rich texture and a fresh, milky flavor. And it makes all the difference.

MAKES ONE 9-INCH LATTICE-TOP TART

TO MAKE THE TART SHELL:

Cut the dough disk into 2 portions, one slightly larger than the other. Rewrap the smaller portion and set aside. On a lightly floured surface, roll out the larger portion into an 11-inch round about ⅛ inch thick or slightly thicker. Carefully wrap the dough around the rolling pin and drape it over a 9-inch fluted tart pan with a removable bottom. Gently press the dough into the bottom and up the sides of the pan. Use the rolling pin or the flat of your hand to press around the perimeter of the pan to cut off any excess dough. Put the lined tart pan in the refrigerator to chill for 30 minutes.

TO MAKE THE FILLING:

In a large bowl, combine the cheese, whole egg and egg yolks, sugar, vanilla, and cinnamon. Using a stand mixer or a handheld mixer, beat the ingredients on high speed for about 1 minute, or until thoroughly combined and fluffy.

Heat the oven to 350 degrees F.

ASSEMBLE AND BAKE THE TART:

Remove the tart shell from the refrigerator. Spoon the filling into the shell and smooth it with a rubber spatula. Roll out the remaining dough portion into a 10-inch round about ⅛ inch thick or slightly thicker, and cut it into ¾-inch-wide strips with a fluted pastry wheel. Carefully place the strips over the filled tart shell in a lattice pattern, gently pressing the ends of the strips into the sides of the tart shell.

Bake the *crostata* for 30 to 40 minutes, or until the crust is golden. Remove the *crostata* from the oven and place it on a wire rack to cool for 20 minutes, or until cool enough to handle. Remove the rim of the tart pan and let the *crostata* cool completely on the rack before transferring it to a decorative serving platter. Dust with confectioners' sugar if you like.

FOR THE TART SHELL
1 batch *Pasta Frolla* (page 156), slightly cooler than room temperature

Unbleached all-purpose flour for dusting work surface

FOR THE FILLING
12 ripe, unblemished apricots

⅓ cup sugar

Juice of ½ lemon

12 sour cherries, pitted

2 tablespoons sugar for garnish

Apricot and Sour Cherry Tart

CROSTATA DI ALBICOCCHE E AMARENE

Apricots and sour cherries, also called pie cherries or tart cherries (Montmorency and Morello are popular varieties), are my favorite summer fruits. Both have a short season that just barely overlaps, so consider it an accomplishment if you are able to get them together in the same tart. The cherries in this crostata are really a garnish, perched inside the apricot halves. If sour cherries are unavailable, use pitted sweet cherries. Later in summer, you can use peaches, nectarines, or plums in place of the apricots.

MAKES ONE 9-INCH TART

TO MAKE THE TART SHELL:
Cut the dough disk into 2 portions, one slightly larger than the other. Rewrap the smaller portion and freeze for up to 1 month to use for making cookies at a later date. On a lightly floured surface, roll out the larger portion into an 11-inch round about ⅛ inch thick or slightly thicker. Carefully wrap the dough around the rolling pin and drape it over a 9-inch fluted tart pan with a removable bottom. Gently press the dough into the bottom and up the sides of the pan. Use the rolling pin or the flat of your hand to press around the perimeter of the pan to cut off any excess dough. Put the lined tart pan in the refrigerator to chill for 30 minutes.

TO MAKE THE FILLING:
Cut the apricots in half and remove and discard their pits. Set aside 12 halves and chop the remaining halves coarsely. Put the chopped apricots in a saucepan with the sugar and lemon juice and bring to a boil over medium heat. Cook, stirring with a wooden spoon, for about 5 minutes, or until the apricots have softened to a jamlike consistency. Remove from the heat and let cool to room temperature. Reserve the cherries for using later.

Heat the oven to 375 degrees F.

CONTINUED

ASSEMBLE AND BAKE THE TART:

Remove the tart shell from the refrigerator. Spoon the cooked apricot mixture into the shell and smooth it with a rubber spatula. Arrange the 12 reserved apricot halves, cut side up, over the mixture, covering the top as evenly as possible. Place a pitted cherry inside the hollow of each half. If all 12 apricot halves don't fit, cut up the extras and use the pieces to fill in any spaces. Sprinkle 2 tablespoons sugar over the fruit.

Bake the *crostata* for 30 to 40 minutes, or until the apricots are tender and the crust is golden brown. Turn off the oven and leave the *crostata* in the oven for 10 minutes. Then remove the *crostata* from the oven and place it on a wire rack to cool for 20 minutes, or until cool enough to handle. Remove the rim of the tart pan and let the *crostata* cool completely on the rack before transferring it to a decorative serving platter.

SOURCES

FOR IMPORTED RIZZOLI ANCHOVIES:

A.G. Ferrari Foods
877-878-2783
www.agferrari.com

Zingerman's Deli
422 Detroit Street
Ann Arbor, MI 48104
888-636-8162
www.zingermans.com

**FOR DRIED BEANS AND OTHER LEGUMES,
DRIED PORCINI MUSHROOMS, SPICES, AND OTHER
IMPORTED ITALIAN INGREDIENTS:**

A.G. Ferrari Foods
877-878-2783
www.agferrari.com

Rafal Spice Company
2521 Russell Street
Detroit, MI 48207
800-228-4276
www.rafalspice.com

**FOR ITALIAN COOKING EQUIPMENT, TART PANS,
CHRISTMAS LIMAS AND OTHER HEIRLOOM DRIED BEANS,
AND OTHER SPECIALTY PRODUCTS:**

La Cuisine: The Cook's Resource
323 Cameron Street
Alexandria, VA 22314
800-521-1176
www.lacuisineus.com

**FOR FRESH RICOTTA AND OTHER
AMERICAN-MADE ITALIAN CHEESES:**

Mozzarella Company
2944 Elm Street
Dallas, TX 75226
214-741-4072;
800-798-2954
www.mozzco.com

INDEX

A

Anchovies, 18
Apple Tart, 157
Apricot and Sour Cherry Tart, 161-62
Artichoke Stew with Lettuce and Peas, 117-18
Asparagus Soup, Cream of, with
    Pearled Barley, 103-4

B

Barley, Pearled, Cream of Asparagus
    Soup with, 103-4
Basic Tomato Sauce, 30
Beans, 18. See also Chickpeas
    Country Vegetable Soup, 49-51
    Cranberry Bean Stew with Fennel and
        Radicchio, 52
    Green Beans Stewed with Tomatoes, 145
    Lamb and Green Bean Stew with Farro, 56
    Pasta and Bean Soup with Christmas
        Limas, 77
    Shepherd's Soup, 101
    Spring Cleaning Soup, 107
    Tuna and White Bean Stew, 134
Beef, 20
    Beef Stew with Juniper Berries, 90-91
    Gabriella's Pot Roast, 115
    Homemade Meat Broth, 26
    Neapolitan Braised Beef with Onions,
        58-59
    Nonna's Chicken Soup, 100
    Olive-Stuffed Meatballs in Light Tomato
        Sauce, 136-37
    Rich Roasted Beef Broth, 25
    Stuffed Beef Roll in Tomato Sauce, 141-43
Bietola con le Patate, 119
Black Pepper Crostini, 148
Black Pepper Croutons, 150
Braised Rapini and Kale, 61
Braised Veal Shanks in Brown Sauce, 88-89
Braising, 17
Bread, 18
    Black Pepper Crostini, 148
    Black Pepper Croutons, 150
    Bread Stick Soup, 41
    Country Vegetable Soup, 49-51

    crumbs, making, 100
    cubes, toasted, 127
    Dumplings in Broth, 72
    Garlic-Rubbed Grilled Bread, 151
    Large Toasted Bread Slices with
        Pecorino, 149
    Poached Egg Soup from Pavia, 99
    Sourdough Croutons, 150
    Toasted Bread Slices, 148
    Whole-Wheat Croutons, 150
    Zia Gilda's Zucchini and Bread Soup, 127
Brodo di Carne, 26
Brodo di Magro, 27
Brodo di Pollo, 24
Broths
    commercial vs. homemade, 23
    Homemade Chicken Broth, 24
    Homemade Meat Broth, 26
    Homemade Vegetable Broth, 27
    Rich Roasted Beef Broth, 25
Browning, 17
Bruschetta, 151
Buckwheat Polenta, 154

C

Calamari
    Christmas Eve Calamari, 79
    thawing frozen, 79
Calamari in Umido per la Vigilia di Natale, 79
Canederli in Brodo, 72
Cappelletti in Brodo per Natale, 69-70
Cheese
    halloumi, 145
    mascarpone, 20
    Parmigiano-Reggiano, 20
    pecorino romano, 20-21
    Ricotta Cheese Tart, 160
    ricotta salata, 52
    toma piemontese, 41
Cherry, Sour, and Apricot Tart, 161-62
Chestnuts, 18
    Chestnut Polenta, 154
    Chickpea and Chestnut Soup, 47-48
    Cream of Chestnut Soup, 42
Chicken, 18

    Chicken in Piquant Tomato Sauce, 55
    Chicken with Eggplant, 140
    Homemade Chicken Broth, 24
    Homemade Meat Broth, 26
    Nonna's Chicken Soup, 100
    Smothered Chicken with Escarole and
        Leeks, 111
    Stuffed Pasta "Hats" in Broth for
        Christmas, 69-70
    Whole Chicken Stewed in Trebbiano, 83
Chickpeas
    Chickpea and Chestnut Soup, 47-48
    Pasta with Chickpeas and Rosemary, 131
    Spring Cleaning Soup, 107
Chopping, 16
Christmas Eve Calamari, 79
Cipolline Glassate, 63
Clams
    Clam Stew with Prosecco, 108
    cleaning, 16
    Curried Shellfish Stew, 53
    Saffron-Scented Fish Stew, 80-81
    storing, 16
Costate di Maiale in Salsa di Pomodoro e
    Porcini, 86-87
Country Vegetable Soup, 49-51
Cracked Farro Soup, 132
Cranberry Bean Stew with Fennel and
    Radicchio, 52
Cream, adding, to soups, 17
Cream of Asparagus Soup with Pearled
    Barley, 103-4
Cream of Chestnut Soup, 42
Creamy Porcini Soup, 43-44
Crema di Castagne, 42
Crema di Piselli alla Maggiorana, 105
Crema di Porcini, 43-44
Crêpes in Broth, 98
Crespelle in Brodo, 98
Crostata di Albicocche e Amarene, 161-62
Crostata di Marmellata, 159
Crostata di Mele, 157
Crostata di Ricotta, 160
Crostini, 148
Crostini al Pepe, 148

Crostoni al Pecorino, 149
Croutons
    Black Pepper Croutons, 150
    Sourdough Croutons, 150
    Whole-Wheat Croutons, 150
Curried Shellfish Stew, 53

D

Dadini di Pane al Pepe, 150
Deglazing, 17
Dinosaur kale, 51
    Country Vegetable Soup, 49–51
Dumplings in Broth, 72

E

Eggplant
    Chicken with Eggplant, 140
    Tubetti with Summer Vegetables, 130
Eggs, 18
    Fresh Egg Pasta Dough, 31–33
    Peppers and Eggs, 144
    Poached Egg Soup from Pavia, 99
Endive, Oven-Braised, 92
Equipment, 14–15
Escarole
    Lettuce and Rice Soup, 106
    Nonna's Chicken Soup, 100
    Smothered Chicken with Escarole and
        Leeks, 111

F

Fagiolini all'Uccelletto, 145
Fagioli Stufati Con Finocchio e Radicchio, 52
Farro, 18
    Cracked Farro Soup, 132
    Lamb and Green Bean Stew with Farro, 56
Fatback, 18, 20
Fennel, 20
    Cranberry Bean Stew with Fennel and
        Radicchio, 52
    Cream of Asparagus Soup with Pearled
        Barley, 103–4
    Fennel-Scented Pork Stew, 57
    seeds, crushing, 57
    Spring Cleaning Soup, 107

Zucchini Blossoms in Summer Broth, 125
Fiori di Zucca in Brodo Estiva, 125
Fish
    Overnight-Marinated Swordfish Stew, 139
    Saffron-Scented Fish Stew, 80–81
    Tuna and White Bean Stew, 134
Fresh Egg Pasta Dough, 31–33
Fresh Tomato Sauce, 28

G

Gabriella's Pot Roast, 115
Gamberetti Piccanti in Umido, 110
Garlic-Rubbed Grilled Bread, 151
Glazed Onions in Cream, 63
Gnocchi, Semolina, in Homemade Meat
    Broth, 39
Gnocchi de Semolina in Brodo di Carne, 39
Grated Pasta Soup, 71
Green Beans Stewed with Tomatoes, 145

H

Herbs
    chopping, 16
    fresh vs. dried, 20
Homemade Chicken Broth, 24
Homemade Meat Broth, 26
Homemade Vegetable Broth, 27

I

Indivia Brasata al Forno, 92

J

Jam Tart, 159

K

Kale and Rapini, Braised, 61

L

La Genovese, 58–59
Lamb, 20
    Lamb and Green Bean Stew with
        Farro, 56
    Lamb and Potato Stew, 113
Large Toasted Bread Slices with Pecorino,
    149

Leeks
    Smothered Chicken with Escarole and
        Leeks, 111
    Sweet Pea Soup with Marjoram, 105
Lentils, 18
    Lentil Soup, 46
    Sausages and Lentils in the Style of
        Umbria, 85
    Spring Cleaning Soup, 107
Lettuce
    Artichoke Stew with Lettuce and Peas, 117–18
    Lettuce and Rice Soup, 106
Lobster
    removing meat from tails of, 81
    Saffron-Scented Fish Stew, 80–81

M

Maccu, 107
Marinating, 16
Marsala, 20
Meatballs
    Nonna's Chicken Soup, 100
    Olive-Stuffed Meatballs in Light Tomato
        Sauce, 136–37
Minestra della Nonna, 100
Minestra del Pastore, 101
Minestra di Ceci e di Castagne, 47–48
Minestra di Lattuga e Riso, 106
Minestra di Pasta Grattata, 71
Mortadella
    Dumplings in Broth, 72
    Stuffed Pasta "Hats" in Broth for
        Christmas, 69–70
Mushrooms
    Braised Veal Shanks in Brown Sauce, 88–89
    Creamy Porcini Soup, 43–44
    porcini, 21
    Pork Ribs in Tomato-Porcini Sauce, 86–87
    Whole Chicken Stewed in Trebbiano, 83
Mussels
    cleaning, 16
    Curried Shellfish Stew, 53
    Mussel Stew with Roasted Peppers, 133
    Saffron-Scented Fish Stew, 80–81
    storing, 16

N

Neapolitan Braised Beef with Onions, 58–59
Nonna's Chicken Soup, 100
Nutmeg, 20

O

Olive oil, 20
Olives
    Chicken with Eggplant, 140
    Olive-Stuffed Meatballs in Light
        Tomato Sauce, 136–37
    Overnight-Marinated Swordfish
        Stew, 139
Onions
    Glazed Onions in Cream, 63
    Neapolitan Braised Beef with Onions,
        58–59
    Onion Soup with Pecorino, 74
Osso Buco in Salsa Bruna, 88–89
Oven-Braised Endive, 92
Overnight-Marinated Swordfish Stew, 139

P

Pancetta, 20
Pancotto con le Zucchine alla Zia Gilda, 127
Pasta
    Fresh Egg Pasta Dough, 31–33
    Grated Pasta Soup, 71
    Neapolitan Braised Beef with Onions,
        58–59
    Nonna's Chicken Soup, 100
    Pasta and Bean Soup with Christmas
        Limas, 77
    Pasta and Potato Soup with Paprika, 76
    Pasta with Chickpeas and Rosemary, 131
    Pastina Cooked in Broth, 11
    Pork Ribs in Tomato-Porcini Sauce, 86–87
    Shepherd's Soup, 101
    Stuffed Pasta "Hats" in Broth for
        Christmas, 69–70
    Tubetti with Summer Vegetables, 130
Pasta all'Uovo, 31–33
Pasta e Ceci al Rosmarino, 131
Pasta e Fagioli Invernale, 77
Pasta e Patate alla Paprika, 76

Pasta Frolla, 156
Pastry Dough, 156
Peas, 18
    Artichoke Stew with Lettuce and Peas,
        117–18
    Shepherd's Soup, 101
    Spring Cleaning Soup, 107
    Sweet Pea Soup with Marjoram, 105
Peperoni e Uova, 144
Peppers
    Mussel Stew with Roasted Peppers, 133
    Peppers and Eggs, 144
    roasting, 133
    September Soup, 128
    Tubetti with Summer Vegetables, 130
    Veal and Pepper Stew, 135
Poached Egg Soup from Pavia, 99
Polenta, 21, 154
    Buckwheat Polenta, 154
    Chestnut Polenta, 154
Polenta di Castagne, 154
Polenta di Frumentino, 154
Pollo alle Melanzane, 140
Pollo in Salsa Piccante, 55
Pollo Stufato con Trebbiano, 83
Polpettine Farcite in Salsa Estiva, 136–37
Pork, 20
    Fennel-Scented Pork Stew, 57
    Nonna's Chicken Soup, 100
    Olive-Stuffed Meatballs in Light Tomato
        Sauce, 136–37
    Pork Ribs in Tomato-Porcini Sauce, 86–87
    Stuffed Pasta "Hats" in Broth for
        Christmas, 69–70
Potatoes
    Country Vegetable Soup, 49–51
    Lamb and Potato Stew, 113
    Pasta and Potato Soup with Paprika, 76
    Shepherd's Soup, 101
    Swiss Chard and Potatoes, 119
    Tubetti with Summer Vegetables, 130
Prosciutto di Parma, 21
    Braised Veal Shanks in Brown Sauce, 88–89
    Chickpea and Chestnut Soup, 47–48
    Stuffed Beef Roll in Tomato Sauce, 141–43

Stuffed Pasta "Hats" in Broth for
    Christmas, 69–70
Whole Chicken Stewed in Trebbiano, 83

R

Radicchio, Cranberry Bean Stew with
    Fennel and, 52
Rapini and Kale, Braised, 61
Rapini e Cavolo Riccio Brasati, 61
Reheating, 17
Ribollita, 49–51
Rice
    Lettuce and Rice Soup, 106
    Saffron Risotto, 152
    Simple Risotto, 152
    varieties of, 18
Rich Roasted Beef Broth, 25
Ricotta Cheese Tart, 160
Risotto
    Saffron Risotto, 152
    Simple Risotto, 152
Risotto allo Zafferano, 152
Risotto Semplice, 152
Rotolo di Manzo Farcito e Brasato, 141–43

S

Saffron, 21
    Saffron Risotto, 152
    Saffron-Scented Fish Stew, 80–81
Salsa Fresca di Pomodoro, 28
Salsa Semplice di Pomodoro, 30
Salsicce e Lenticchie all'Umbriana, 85
Salt, 21
Sauces
    Basic Tomato Sauce, 30
    Fresh Tomato Sauce, 28
Sausages and Lentils in the Style of
    Umbria, 85
Sautéing, 16
Seasoning, 17
Semolina flour, 21
Semolina Gnocchi in Homemade Meat
    Broth, 39
September Soup, 128
Shepherd's Soup, 101

Shrimp
  Curried Shellfish Stew, 53
  peeling and deveining, 16
  Saffron-Scented Fish Stew, 80–81
  Spicy Shrimp Stew, 110
Simmering, 17
Simple Risotto, 152
Smothered Chicken with Escarole and
      Leeks, 111
Sostanzioso Brodo di Manzo, 25
Sourdough Croutons, 150
Spezzatino al Ginepro, 90–91
Spezzatino di Agnello con Fagiolini e Farro, 56
Spezzatino di Agnello e Patate, 113
*Spezzatino di Maiale al Sapore di
      Finocchio*, 57
Spezzatino di Vitello con i Peperoni, 135
Spicy Shrimp Stew, 110
Spinach
  Lettuce and Rice Soup, 106
  Nonna's Chicken Soup, 100
Spring Cleaning Soup, 107
Squid. *See* Calamari
Stewing, 17
Storing, 17
Stracotto di Manzo alla Gabriella, 115
Stufato di Carciofi con Lattuga e Piselli,
      117–18
Stufato di Pesce Spada, 139
Stufato di Pollo con Scarola e Porri, 111
Stuffed Beef Roll in Tomato Sauce, 141–43
Stuffed Pasta "Hats" in Broth for Christmas,
      69–70
Sweet Pea Soup with Marjoram, 105
Swiss chard, 119
Spring Cleaning Soup, 107
Swiss Chard and Potatoes, 119
Swordfish Stew, Overnight-Marinated, 139

T
Tarts
  Apple Tart, 157
  Apricot and Sour Cherry Tart, 161–62
  Jam Tart, 159
  Ricotta Cheese Tart, 160

Techniques, 16–17
Toasted Bread Slices, 148
Tomatoes
  Basic Tomato Sauce, 30
  canned, 21
  Chicken in Piquant Tomato Sauce, 55
  Chicken with Eggplant, 140
  Christmas Eve Calamari, 79
  Country Vegetable Soup, 49–51
  Cranberry Bean Stew with Fennel and
        Radicchio, 52
  Fennel-Scented Pork Stew, 57
  Fresh Tomato Sauce, 28
  Gabriella's Pot Roast, 115
  Green Beans Stewed with Tomatoes, 145
  Lamb and Green Bean Stew with Farro, 56
  Lamb and Potato Stew, 113
  Mussel Stew with Roasted Peppers, 133
  Olive-Stuffed Meatballs in Light Tomato
        Sauce, 136–37
  Oven-Braised Endive, 92
  Overnight-Marinated Swordfish Stew, 139
  Pasta and Potato Soup with Paprika, 76
  Pasta with Chickpeas and Rosemary, 131
  peeling and seeding, 16
  Peppers and Eggs, 144
  Pork Ribs in Tomato-Porcini Sauce, 86–87
  Saffron-Scented Fish Stew, 80–81
  September Soup, 128
  Stuffed Beef Roll in Tomato Sauce, 141–43
  Tuna and White Bean Stew, 134
Tonno e Cannellini in Salsa, 134
Tubetti con Verdura Estiva, 130
Tubetti with Summer Vegetables, 130
Tuna and White Bean Stew, 134

V
Veal, 20
  Braised Veal Shanks in Brown Sauce,
        88–89
  Nonna's Chicken Soup, 100
  Olive-Stuffed Meatballs in Light Tomato
        Sauce, 136–37
  Stuffed Pasta "Hats" in Broth for
        Christmas, 69–70

Veal and Pepper Stew, 135
Vegetables. *See also individual vegetables*
  chopping, 16
  Country Vegetable Soup, 49–51
  Homemade Vegetable Broth, 27
  Tubetti with Summer Vegetables, 130
Vellutata di Asparagi con Orzo Perlato,
      103–4

W
Water, 21
White Wine Soup, 73
Whole Chicken Stewed in Trebbiano, 83
Whole-Wheat Croutons, 150
Wine, 21
  Clam Stew with Prosecco, 108
  White Wine Soup, 73
  Whole Chicken Stewed in Trebbiano, 83

Z
Zia Gilda's Zucchini and Bread Soup, 127
Zucchini
  Tubetti with Summer Vegetables, 130
  Zia Gilda's Zucchini and Bread Soup, 127
  Zucchini Blossoms in Summer Broth, 125
Zuppa alla Pavese, 99
Zuppa al Vino Bianco, 73
Zuppa di Cipolle al Pecorino, 74
Zuppa di Cozze con Peperoni Arrosti, 133
Zuppa di Frutti di Mare al Farouk, 53
Zuppa di Grissini, 41
Zuppa di Lenticchie, 46
Zuppa di Magro alla Campagnola, 49–51
Zuppa di Pesce allo Zafferano, 80–81
Zuppa di Vongole al Prosecco, 108
Zuppa per Settembre, 128
Zuppetta di Farro Spezzetato, 132

TABLE OF EQUIVALENTS

The exact equivalents in the following tables have been rounded for convenience.

LIQUID/DRY MEASURES

U.S.	METRIC
¼ teaspoon	1.25 milliliters
½ teaspoon	2.5 milliliters
1 teaspoon	5 milliliters
1 tablespoon (3 teaspoons)	15 milliliters
1 fluid ounce (2 tablespoons)	30 milliliters
¼ cup	60 milliliters
⅓ cup	80 milliliters
½ cup	120 milliliters
1 cup	240 milliliters
1 pint (2 cups)	480 milliliters
1 quart (4 cups, 32 ounces)	960 milliliters
1 gallon (4 quarts)	3.84 liters
1 ounce (by weight)	28 grams
1 pound	454 grams
2.2 pounds	1 kilogram

LENGTH

U.S.	METRIC
⅛ inch	3 millimeters
¼ inch	6 millimeters
½ inch	12 millimeters
1 inch	2.5 centimeters

OVEN TEMPERATURE

FAHRENHEIT	CELSIUS	GAS
250	120	½
275	140	1
300	150	2
325	160	3
350	180	4
375	190	5
400	200	6
425	220	7
450	230	8
475	240	9
500	260	10